# THE HAPPY COUPLE'S HANDBOOK

## Powerful Life Hacks for a Successful Relationship

ANDREW G. MARSHALL

MARSHALL METHOD
PUBLISHING

Every reasonable effort has been made to contact copyright holders. If any have been overlooked, the publishers would be glad to hear from them and make good in future editions any errors or omissions brought to their attention.

The case histories in this book are based on couples with whom I have worked in my marital therapy practice (their identities have been changed to protect confidentiality and sometimes two or three cases have been merged together) and individuals who wrote to my website.

If readers have a medical complaint, it is important that they consult their doctor.

**Marshall Method Publishing**
London • Florida • Berlin
www.marshallmethodpublishing.com

**Library of Congress Cataloging-in-Publication Date is available through the Library of Congress.**

ISBN: 978-0-9955403-7-8

Cover and interior design: Gary A. Rosenberg • www.thebookcouple.com

Printed in the United States of America

10   9   8   7   6   5   4   3   2   1

*To Heather,*
*for all her work behind the scenes*

# Contents

# Introduction

Wouldn't it wonderful if the night before you got married, someone tapped you on the shoulder and told you all the secrets of a happy marriage? Ideally, it would be your mother or your father but sadly nobody initiated them into how to nurture, protect, and repair their love either. They had to make it up as they went along too.

If you were lucky, your parents had good instincts and created a loving atmosphere that has helped you grow and thrive. Yet even in these circumstances, they would probably find it hard to offer any advice—because when things are working well, there is no need to look under the hood and understand what makes a relationship run smoothly.

If you were unlucky, your parents had a tough start in life—perhaps their parents died when they were young, hardships meant everybody was too busy surviving, or there were dark family secrets—and although your mother and father have done their best for you, they have nothing more to offer than "don't make the same mistakes I did."

Nobody told me the secrets on the eve of my marriage either. Although my parents were happily married for fifty-nine years, my father was a man of few words. He could have explained how to balance my accounts or how to hang wallpaper but not what makes a relationship tick. My mother was equally practical and, when I was growing up, nobody ever discussed feelings. No wonder I became a therapist and spend my life talking about them!

The most important thing I've learned from my training, working with over three thousand clients, and from my own personal experience is that love needs skills as well as chemistry. So what are these skills? They are about naming your feelings and reporting them—rather than being overwhelmed by them or bottling them up and then blowing. I will teach you to ask for what you need—rather than dropping hints or nagging until your partner finally complies. I will help you to say "no" or "maybe" and to negotiate with your partner. I will explain the rules for a good argument—where you can disagree and resolve issues without hurting each other. In effect, I will initiate you into the secrets of a happy marriage and teach you the skills that your parents either didn't know or couldn't put into words.

Perhaps this sounds like a lot of hard work, but don't worry. I have boiled down everything I've gleaned in over thirty years of counseling couples into a set of simple life hacks. (My thanks to everyone who has allowed me to use their experiences to write this book. I have changed some of the details to protect identities and in some cases blended stories.) I believe that small changes can make a big difference to your relationship. My policy is not to ask you to work harder but to think smarter so your relationship will become more connected and more loving.

Finally, if your marriage is hanging by a thread or you're recovering from infidelity—and you want to stay together but you don't know how—these life hacks are powerful enough to repair the damage.

Whatever your situation, it's never too late to learn the skills for a happy marriage. So please consider this book your tap on the shoulder …

Andrew G. Marshall
www.andrewgmarshall.com

# CHAPTER ONE

<br>

# Taking Stock

What is the best predictor of a long and happy relationship? Coming from similar backgrounds? Common interests, ambitions, and attitudes? A healthy sex life? The amount of support from family and friends? Great chemistry? All of these are useful, but ultimately not decisive. Numerous research projects have come to the same conclusion. It doesn't matter how many problems a couple face, or how difficult, the best predictor for happiness is how well they are handled.

It should be reasonably easy to disagree with your partner, put your point of view across, debate the differences, and find a compromise. After all, you love each other and want the best for each other. But this is just one of the many paradoxes about love. The more that you love someone, the more it hurts if he or she is upset and the more you hurt if he or she rejects you. So while a dispute with a work colleague or a run-in with a stranger can be shrugged off reasonably easily, one with your partner is doubly painful and therefore doubly difficult to resolve.

Worse still, there are no lessons at school on how to argue effectively and make up afterward—so there is no resentment and fuel for round two—and if you did not learn at home (because your parents set the negative example of sulking for days or tearing into each other) it is even harder to know where to start. That's why I have put together a series of love hacks to draw on. It will help you foster attitudes that take the sting out of disagreements, recognize any bad habits, put your case in an assertive but not aggressive way, listen to your partner respectfully, postmortem a row, and ultimately, resolve your differences.

The first love hack is to take stock and understand how you and your partner settle disputes.

## WHAT'S YOUR ARGUING STYLE?

This quiz puts the spotlight on your relationship's strengths and weaknesses, and provides some targeted advice:

1. You partner leaves her or his shoes where you can trip over them, or clothes where they don't belong. What is your reaction?

   a) Count to ten.

   b) My partner is thoughtless, lazy, or disrespectful.

   c) I really must speak to him or her.

2. Your partner needs to spend time away from home for his or her job, hobby, or further education. This leaves you looking after the kids—again. How do you react?

   a) Inwardly seethe and feel taken for granted. However, you complain only to your mother, a friend, or not at all.

   b) Get your revenge by being uncooperative or by coming up with lots of obstacles.

   c) You agree but ask him or her to cover a night out with your friends in return.

3. What is the unofficial motto of your relationship?

   a) Don't make waves.

   b) When it's good it's very, very good and when it's bad it's horrid.

   c) Together we can take on the world.

4. Your partner has an irritating habit—such as slurping coffee. What do you about it?

   a) Sigh. You've spoken about it before.

   b) Make a sarcastic comment.

   c) Ask her or him to wait until it's not so hot.

5. You make an amorous advance in bed but your partner is not really in the mood and would prefer a cuddle instead. How do you react?

   a) Have a half-hearted cuddle but privately resolve not to risk rejection in the future.

   b) Turn your back and make him or her feel guilty or know how it feels to be turned down.

   c) Enjoy the cuddle but talk about it the next day and explain how upset you felt.

6. You are in the car together and you're lost, late, and tired. What happens next?

   a) You sulk and finish the journey in silence.

   b) Your partner complains about your map reading and you blame him or her for taking the wrong turning.

   c) You ask for directions.

7. Your partner arranges for her or his parents, who you can cope with only in small doses, to visit for a long weekend without asking. What is your reaction?

   a) Invite friends round to lessen the burden and help the weekend go smoothly.

   b) Get angry and have it out.

   c) Explain why the decision hurts and what would make it easier.

8.  It's a hot summer's day and an attractive man or woman walks past wearing very little. What do you do?

    a)  Pretend not to notice as it avoids a nasty row.

    b)  Check your partner is not ogling them and get upset if she or he looks twice.

    c)  Tease each other or point out the beautiful stranger's failings.

9.  Your electricity bill is huge. What happens next?

    a)  Each of you makes a couple of pointed comments over the next few days about lights left on.

    b)  You accuse each other of being wasteful and bring up other bad habits.

    c)  You agree on a plan for saving energy and money.

10. Which of the following do your arguments most closely resemble?

    a)  An on/off switch. Either one or the other of you wants to talk or is annoyed, but seldom both at the same time.

    b)  Cat and dog fight. Lots of rough-and-tumble with both sides losing their temper.

    c)  A debating chamber. Although things can get heated, everybody gets their say.

---

**MOSTLY a): Low-conflict:** The two of you get on well enough and life runs smoothly, but there is very little passion. Sometimes, it can seem that you are more brother and sister than husband and wife. Don't panic, it is possible to get the passion back. The first step is to admit to the problem and the second to stop sidestepping things that irritate you or pretending that they don't matter. Contrary to popular opinion, arguing is good for your relationship. It sorts out what is truly important and creates a sense that something needs to change. Expressing anger, making up, and finally sorting out a compromise is the most intimate thing a couple can do. Isn't it time you showed your partner that you care? (You will find Chapter Four particularly helpful.)

**MOSTLY b): High-conflict:** There is plenty of passion in your relationship, but is it always positive? Although you are not afraid to let rip, the rows just tend to push you and your partner into separate corners rather than solving anything. When you're upset, the automatic response is to punish—either by withdrawing or criticizing. Guess what? Your partner will sink down to your level and the relationship becomes trapped in a negative downward spiral. Why not lead by example and do something nice instead? Your partner might not immediately respond in kind, but before long he or she will feel better disposed and ready to return the favor. Miracle of miracles, you have set up a positive circle. It just takes somebody to make the first move. Why not you? Don't expect your partner to change overnight; in fact she or he will probably be suspicious, but be patient. After three or four weeks, you should see a difference. With your relationship on an even keel, you are ready to discuss what went wrong. (You will find Chapter Five particularly useful.)

**MOSTLY c): Medium-conflict:** You don't overreact to problems and you don't ignore them. Congratulations for finding the middle path. However, be wary, especially if you answered "a" or "b" to some questions, as certain topics or being tired and stressed can still overwhelm your arguing skills. Under these circumstances, the atmosphere at home can easily turn from happy into dissatisfied. Probably about thirty percent of couples who seek my help have medium-conflict relationships. (You will find Chapter Seven, "How to Argue Effectively," particularly helpful, but please read the other chapters to understand how arguments can turn sour.)

# THE PARADOX OF LOVE

The more we love our partner, the more important his or her love becomes and the more frightened we are of losing it. So we worry that if we don't do what our partner wants then he or she will reject us. Conversely if our partner does not go along with what we want or think is for the best, we can begin to question if she or he truly loves us. It is not surprising that small things can quickly escalate and the stakes become sky high.

So how do we deal with different tastes, standards, and attitudes? Every relationship faces this problem, partly because no two people are alike, but mainly because we are programmed to choose a partner who has the qualities we lack. In the best case scenario, these differences are catalysts for growth rather than conflict.

However, difference can become so threatening that each partner will adopt strategies to either sidestep the problem or take charge and get their own way. Nobody sets out to be either controlling or a doormat—they just get frightened. Here comes the central paradox: almost everything we do is to protect us from pain, but most of the pain comes from this protective behavior.

Here are five major patterns that couples adopt to deal with their differences:

## Control/Compliance

One partner is in charge and the other falls in with their wishes. From traditional sitcoms, we would immediately recognize the overbearing wife and the timid husband. However, in real relationships, it is often more complex with couples swapping control and capitulating over different issues. For example, with Martin, a thirty-two-year-old truck driver, and his partner, Jackie a twenty-eight-year-old office manager, he was in charge of their social life. Martin would hold court with their group of friends, decide how long they stayed, and generally where and with whom they spent their leisure time. Jackie would go along with his wishes. However, Jackie controlled almost everything in the home—the budget, where everything was kept, what they ate, when and how they cleaned up—and Martin would fall in with these dictates. Some couples can rub along with these tight demarcations for years, until something breaks down the walls. In the case of Martin and Jackie, it was the arrival of a baby. She found herself overwhelmed at home and he found the restrictions on their social life impossible.

Control is also more complex than just ordering somebody about or physically intimidating them. Sometimes to the outside world, the half that seems the weaker is actually very controlling. Some of the techniques to take charge, without seeming to, include: angry tears, "poor me" tears, illness, threats of leaving, guilt-inducing body language (like sighing, raised eyebrows, shrugging shoulders), blame, accusations, and lectures. Although this list makes Control/Compliance seem exhausting, in most cases the behavior can provide a superficial peaceful coexistence. However, the compliant partner will feel more relaxed and spontaneous when the controlling partner is not around. Certainly, Martin felt he could truly relax at home only when Jackie was not in. Meanwhile, Jackie felt more herself—and certainly not watching every word for fear of upstaging Martin—on the rare occasions that she went out with her girlfriends.

## Indifference/Indifference

These relationships are deceptively calm with few lows or highs. The two lives run side by side, in parallel, but the couple have given up wanting much from each other. These relationships were common in the first half of the twentieth century when the vast majority put most emphasis on survival of the marriage and considered their personal happiness less important. The modern equivalent of indifference—withdrawing both emotionally and physically—is the workaholic relationship. Here one partner might claim to want more couple time, but always has an excuse for a few more hours on the computer. Rather than challenging this behavior, their partner gets on with his or her life. Other distancing behavior includes: watching television, getting drunk, sport, and burying oneself in hobbies.

Generally, with Indifference/Indifference there is little talk, no intimacy, and plenty of boredom. These couples tell me: "We have little in common but the kids." Peter and Nancy had been married for twenty years, but Nancy complained, "I don't feel I really know Peter, he seems withdrawn all the time." While Peter countered, "What's the point in talking? All we ever discuss is work and other people." By avoiding conflict, they had never really opened up on the issues that would let them understand each other better. Although both "indifference" partners will have strong separate identities, there is no couple identity. Especially after the children become less central in their lives, one half of these couples will find the loneliness unbearable. Remember, deep down nobody is truly indifferent. Someone might pretend, or give the appearance of not caring. However, everybody wants to be loved.

## Compliance/Compliance

These are the relationships where both partners are so keen to make each other happy that they both give up their individuality for a couple identity. Kate and David not only worked for the same company, but also sat beside each other in the staff canteen at lunchtime. When I asked if they ever thought of sitting with their individual work colleagues for a change, they both admitted being bored with the current arrangement. "It would be so nice to chat with other people," said Kate, "and then I'd have something to tell David in the evening." David put it slightly differently but came to the same conclusions. So why hadn't he said anything? "I thought it was what Kate wanted," David explained and Kate nodded.

Compliance might seem like the best way to run a relationship; after all, the ability to compromise is essential for a happy partnership. But these couples are so frightened of difference, and therefore so defensive, that they ignore any painful feelings. In other relationships the pain would turn to anger and a row. If Kate and David had argued, one of them would have probably blurted out: "Don't crowd in on me at lunchtime."

## Control/Control

Each half of the couple wants to change the other and even small issues become a power struggle. There are lots of threats and name-calling and ugly opinions pour out in the middle of an argument. Each partner believes that if only the other followed their plan, everything would be fine. When one partner is winning, he or she feels powerful and vindicated but the other partner knows all their weak spots and it is not long before the roles are reversed.

Christina and Fabio had an explosive relationship. It had started as a very passionate affair but day-to-day living—when their differences could no longer be ignored—became impossible. In counseling, they spent a whole session fighting about the best way to stack a dishwasher and the pros and cons of prewash rinsing. When I asked what the argument was really about, Fabio replied: "She wants to control me." He had hardly finished the sentence before Christina leaped in: "What about you? You get upset if I wear anything even remotely sexy. I feel like a teenage daughter having to pass a clothes check before I go out." Straightaway, they were into another round of fighting.

Although the periods when these couples kiss and make up provide a high, the periods when they are fighting are a terrible low. For this reason, Control/Control couples are forever splitting up and getting back together again—sometimes for years on end. It seems they can't live together but can't live without each other. To break this cycle, each partner has to understand the source of their anger, show their vulnerability—rather than masking it with anger—and learn ways of lowering the temperature on their rows.

## Control/Rebellion

One half is valiantly trying to change the other; the other is valiantly trying to resist. Although the frustration is as great as for Control/Control couples, the atmosphere—at least on the surface—is much calmer. This is because the rebelling partner will agree to the plans of the controlling partner but then go out of the way to subvert them.

Olivia wanted a new kitchen and as her husband, Ian, was a builder, it should have been reasonably straightforward. Although Ian agreed in principle, he had many private reservations. He did not want to spend his free time working. He thought his wife's choice was too expensive and he saw nothing wrong with their existing kitchen (which was only three years old). Instead of being honest and giving his true opinions, he sidestepped a possible disagreement and agreed to start "soon." Except, next weekend there was an important baseball game or football match. Futhermore, he spent some of their savings—without consultation—replacing his work van and put off purchasing the kitchen units.

When Olivia's frustration reached fever pitch, he made a start and bought himself some time, but did not follow through. "The kitchen looks like a bomb site," complained Olivia. "But everything's still working," countered Ian, "I'll get round to it—just give me time. And it's not as if I feel encouraged by the atmosphere in the house." Later, in counseling, he admitted he would sometimes pick an argument so he could storm out of the house and avoid the job.

At first glance, Ian might have seemed powerful but it was all negative power. He could just thwart Olivia's desires but he was so busy digging in his heels he had lost sight of what he wanted himself. (This behavior is called Passive Aggression and there is more about this in Chapter Four.) To resolve this pattern, the rebelling partner needs to realize that although he or she might avoid a row in the short term, this strategy causes much more aggravation in the medium and long term. Meanwhile, the controlling partner has to learn to be more flexible. After many weeks discussion, Olivia agreed to cheaper units—rather than her dream kitchen—and they negotiated a works schedule that suited both of them (not just Olivia).

## THE ALTERNATIVE

In small doses, there is nothing wrong with any of these patterns for dealing with difference. Sometimes it is necessary for one half to make a decision and the other to go along with it (Control/Compliance) or to row about important issues (Control/Control). Likewise, there are times when neither partner has the energy or inclination to get worked up over something (Indifference/Indifference). The problem is when a couple becomes stuck in one particular pattern or, worse still, retreats into more and more extreme versions. In the long term this behavior will drain all the connection, all the understanding, and ultimately, all the love out of a relationship.

Fortunately, there is an alternative: Open and honest communication—which leads to Cooperation/Cooperation.

## THREE LAWS OF RELATIONSHIP DISPUTES

Before you can reach Cooperation/Cooperation, I need to lay out three fundamental ideas that will lower the stakes in your arguments, build bridges, and explain why seemingly small issues can become major sticking points.

### All Arguments are "Six of One and Half a Dozen of the Other"

This wisdom was always my mother's response when my sister and I fell out and tried to get her to take sides. In over thirty years of relationship counseling, I have yet to meet a couple that did not share equal responsibility for their problems. (The exception is violent and abusive relationships or when someone is an addict.) From time to time, I hear such a persuasive story that I've been tempted to believe I've finally found an exception. However, with a little digging, I always find that the story is not so black and white. Both sides have made an equal, if different, contribution to their unhappiness.

Unfortunately, our culture, and particularly the law, is determined to divide the innocent from the guilty. When we tell our friends, "You'll never believe what he said to me" or "Guess what she's done now," we edit the story for us to appear in the best possible light. We do not mention that we were two inches from our partner's face screaming at the top of our voice, or conveniently forget our own mean and inconsiderate acts. As we reconstruct the fight, either in our heads or to anyone who will listen, we become more in the right and our partner more in the wrong. This process might make it easier for us to live with ourselves, but harder to live with each other.

What about adultery? Is that also six of one and half a dozen of the other? Certainly after an affair, society likes to label the "guilty" party who cheated and the "innocent" party who was cheated on. Yet in my experience, even here the circumstances are always much murkier. When Donna had an affair at work and her husband Elijah found out, she was deeply ashamed and they came into counseling. "What Elijah won't listen to is the reasons why I felt tempted," explained Donna. "He had been so busy that it seemed he paid me no attention whatsoever. When this man at work noticed me, it was very tempting. He even seemed interested in what I was saying." Before anything happened, Donna tried to talk to Elijah and plan more activities together, but Elijah's most important contract was up for renewal. Tied up with his work, Elijah did not even notice that she had embarked on an affair. Donna found this particularly upsetting: "I'd make this extra special effort whenever I went out, and of course I was going out more often. My moods were all over the place— excited one minute, horrified with myself the next. Yet still Elijah didn't twig." Eventually she confessed to the affair and it ended. What Donna did was wrong, but Elijah's behavior was a contributing factor. Innocent? Guilty? Can anyone truly apportion blame? And ultimately, does it matter?

When all the "buts," "ifs," and "extenuating circumstances" have been stripped away, the responsibility in every relationship dispute is pretty much fifty/fifty. Maybe someone could claim forty-eight/ fifty-two, but a generosity of spirit—a very good asset in a relationship—would suggest that it is pointless to quibble.

Once "six of one and half a dozen of the other" has been taken on board, couples are much less likely to fall into the trap of blaming during a nasty argument. After all, both halves have contributed to the problem.

## EXERCISE  SIX OF ONE AND HALF A DOZEN OF THE OTHER

Naturally, it is easier to spot when other couples are equally to blame than to accept equal responsibility in our own relationship. So while getting the hang of this idea, take a break from examining your life and look at a couple from a favorite TV show, book, or movie.

For example, what about Rhett Butler and Scarlet O'Hara in *Gone With the Wind,* Mr. Darcy and Elizabeth Bennett in the UK classic *Pride and Prejudice,* or Charlotte Bronte's Jane Eyre and Mr. Rochester? From the sitcom *Friends,* examine the responsibility of Rachel and Ross or Chandler and Monica.

After a while, spotting the "six of one and half a dozen of the other" for famous couples becomes easy; when this is the case start applying the same test to your own relationship.

## Emotional Equals Attract

When I trained as a relationship counselor, I had found this idea of emotional equals attracting hard to accept. Surely, in every relationship, one person is better at talking about their feelings, and doesn't that make them potentially better skilled with emotions? It is certainly a widespread belief that one half of a partnership—normally a woman—is better at relationships. On many occasions one partner will bring the other with the implicit message—which is sometimes spelled out in the counseling room: "I'm fine, it's him/her who needs sorting out." Yet it soon becomes obvious that both partners need the sessions—equally.

To explain the second law, it is important to understand what makes up an emotionally healthy individual. The first factor is an ability to be honest about and engage with feelings. Every family has its own problem topics handed down from one generation to the next—subjects that the family are so uncomfortable about that each member pretends do not exist. Common examples would be sex, anger, money, competitiveness, sibling rivalry, jealousy—but the list is endless.

"When I was growing up, my mother would get all flustered whenever there was kissing on the TV," said Terry, a twenty-nine-year-old plumber, "and although I'd tease her about it, I've never really felt comfortable talking about sex, and unlike mates at work would never brag about conquests or make dirty jokes. It just doesn't feel right."

Obviously, being human, it is impossible to cut ourselves from complicated emotions, so we ignore them. I think of it as like putting a screen up to hide an unpleasant view. As a rule of thumb, the fewer emotions hidden behind the screen, the more emotionally healthy the individual. Some people have low screens and find it easier to look behind at the difficult emotions; others have such high and thick screens that they are totally unaware of their off-limits subjects.

The second factor for emotional health is well-balanced boundaries. In some families, everybody is so in and out of each other's business that it becomes hard to know what problems or emotions belong to which family member. These low boundaries can be a problem as these children can grow into adults who do not respect their partner's need for privacy or grasp that he or she might have different viewpoints. Conversely, there are some families where the boundaries are so high that the members share virtually nothing; and these children grow into adults who shut their partners out.

On many occasions, someone who appears very good at talking about relationships turns out to be happy with only a narrow range of emotions. Meanwhile, their partner—who talks less but thinks deeper—could find it easier to delve into the difficult topics hidden behind the screen. Alternatively, the silent partner might be better at listening. Whatever the different skills, screens, and boundaries each half of the couple brings to the relationship, each, in fact, has a matching level of emotional maturity. Often the skills are complementary and the secret of relationship counseling is to get a couple pulling in the same direction.

An example of a relationship that seemed, on the surface, to be emotionally unbalanced is Carrie and Jay—in their fifties with two grownup children. Carrie did most of the talking and whenever I asked Jay a question he would either shrug or tell me: "I don't know." That would be Carrie's cue for a long discussion of Jay's mother, his childhood, and what he was feeling. Jay would sit there nodding. Carrie was certainly fluent in the language of feelings but became increasingly uncomfortable when the spotlight was turned onto her. Out of her mouth would come a barrage of words but afterward when I looked at my notes it seemed she had said nothing concrete. So instead I asked Jay to talk about Carrie's background and slowly a few facts emerged. "Carrie's mother was ill for much of her childhood and she used to lie on a divan in the living room," he explained. "I became her eyes and ears," Carrie chipped in. Slowly they painted a picture of a little girl who would listen for hours to her mother's complaints and be her permanently on-call agony aunt. Carrie would also bring snippets of news from the family and neighborhood and they would pore over the details together. "It made me feel important, OK," explained a more subdued Carrie.

Conversely, Jay came from a family where nobody ever talked about feelings. No wonder Carrie and Jay were attracted to each other. Jay found someone to discuss those forbidden feelings and Carrie found a partner for her ventriloquism act. This relationship had worked well at the beginning but Carrie had become more expressive and Jay quieter until—as often is the case—both started hating the other for the very quality that first attracted them.

Finally, it was a question from Jay that proved the breakthrough: "Did you and your mother ever talk about your relationship?" Carrie blustered. I kept quiet. "It can't have been fun stuck inside with your mother when the other girls were out playing," Jay added thoughtfully. Carrie had often analyzed the family, but there were unspoken limits. Her own relationship with her mother, and the restraints it placed on Carrie, were completely taboo. Although Jay might have been more detached from his family, the distance had sharpened his perception. Both Carrie and Jay had their emotional strengths and weaknesses—in effect, equals had attracted.

"Emotional equals attract" is a very difficult philosophy to accept.

I remember explaining it to a journalist who became very thoughtful. "So what does it say about me that I've just had a short relationship with someone needy and paranoid?" she asked. I wished I had kept quiet. However, she decided to answer her own question: "After my divorce, I suppose needy and paranoid just about summed me up." Many other people would have found it easier to blame the ex-partner than look at themselves. Yet blaming our partner makes us disrespectful and cruel toward them, and ultimately produces destructive belittling arguments.

Understanding that emotional equals attracts makes people less likely to belittle each other. After all, each partner has just as many failings—and strengths—as the other.

## EXERCISE   EMOTIONAL EQUALS ATTRACT

When something is hard to take on trust, it is a good idea to find evidence from your life experience. This exercise will help you explore the concept and provide a launch pad for thinking about your own relationship.

- Choose a couple that you know very well and have a chance to watch regularly. If your parents are still together, that would be ideal, but your partner's parents, a sibling and their partner, or a pair of friends will work equally well.

- Take a piece of paper, divide it in half, and at the top of each half write the name of one of the partners.

- Think of all the qualities that make for good relationships: expressive of feelings; keeps things in proportion; good listener; open to change; well-maintained boundaries; insightful; brave; forgiving; thoughtful; assertive; willing to compromise; affectionate; curious; good with compliments; self-aware; kind; ambitious; outgoing; and reliable in a crisis.

- Allocate each quality above—and any more you come up

with—under each partner's name. If both partners demonstrate the quality, put it down for both of them.

- If you wish, you can add character defects too—but this is not essential.

- Compare both halves. How well balanced are the couple? Does the partner who seems to have less on their list have any hidden qualities that are harder to spot?

## The Eighty/Twenty Rule

The stubborn issues that are really hard to resolve are nearly always eighty percent about the past and only twenty percent about today. This is because patterns set up in our childhood have a knock-on effect on our adult relationships. When Kitty passed her driving test in her mid-twenties, she could not understand why her partner's inability to drive became such a big issue. "It had never bothered me before," she said. However, when introduced to the idea that arguments can have roots back to childhood, Kitty began to make connections. "My dad started losing his sight when I was about three; in fact my earliest memory was of his car being towed away after a nasty accident. From then onward, my mother did all the driving and there were times when naturally she resented always being the one on sodas at parties." For Kitty, her partner automatically leaping into the passenger seat had triggered past associations. Once she understood her feelings and explained them to her partner, driving became less of a flash point.

Another example of the Eighty/Twenty rule are Brian and Andy—a gay couple for whom taste and design caused rifts. They were most likely to fight over purchasing something for their house. The twenty percent was about a natural fibers rug for the living room, but the eighty percent was about their backgrounds and their families' attitudes to money. Andy had been brought up in a middle-class family where money was always plentiful, until his father's drinking habits got out of control and the business failed. From this experience,

Andy learned to enjoy money while it was around. Meanwhile, Brian had come from a working-class family—with six brothers and sisters—where, although his father had a steady job, money was always tight. One of his strongest childhood memories was finding money on the beach, the pleasure of being able to give it to his mother, and the extra food it brought that week. Brian's lesson from his childhood was that money is scarce and should be hoarded. Although understanding the Eighty/Twenty rule did not settle whether Brian and Andy should have bought the rug, it did stop the dispute getting out of control or going endlessly round in circles.

Understanding the Eighty/Twenty rule will stop the same issues repeatedly coming up and an argument descending into bitterness.

## **EXERCISE**   THE EIGHTY/TWENTY RULE

This concept is easier to come to grips with than the other exercises, so we will start closer to home.

- **Make a list of the petty things about your partner that irritate you.** For example: hanging around the house without getting dressed on their day off, winding up the dog, or leaving bills lying around the hallway.

- **Now, turn Sherlock Holmes on yourself and discover why these issues get your goat.** What does each bad habit mean to you? What memories does each bring back? What would your mother or father say about these things? What would your previous boyfriends, girlfriends, or partners have said?

- **Next, think back to your childhood and come up with your earliest memory.** How many details can you remember: where were you standing; who else was there; what colors; what smells; any tastes; what about touching something; how did you feel? Once the memory is as vivid as possible, look for other childhood moments that might link in.

- **Still playing detective, start to put together a case.** Remember how detectives first try out a theory, mentally exploring the possibilities and then looking for evidence either to support the theory or knock it down. Take the same approach with the influences of parents on your personality and your relationship issues. For example, Kitty—whose father lost his sight—could discover how frightening her first memory had been. At three, we are very dependent on our parents. She could then ask what impact this had on her choice of partners. Does she play safe with a very reliable man? Conversely, she might need to keep confronting her fears and choose the excitement of a dangerous man. Do not close down any line of inquiry without thinking it through and testing your gut reaction. This is hard, because we are naturally loyal to our parents, but the aim is to understand ourselves, not to blame them.

- **Finally, think back to your parents' favorite sayings.** They might be philosophical, for example: "Life's not fair," or "Do as you would be done by," and "There's no such word as can't." Conversely, they might be personal: "Why can't you be more like your brother?" or "Big boys don't cry," and "Don't worry, you're the _____ one (fill in the gap: pretty, clever, etc.)." Look at how much the drip, drip, drip of these sayings has marked your personality or view of the world. How many of the contentious issues with your partner are built on these opinions? Are they still true?

These questions will help you pinpoint the hidden eighty percent of a current issue with your partner to which you might previously have been oblivious.

# WHERE YOU ARGUE AND WHAT IT SAYS ABOUT YOUR RELATIONSHIP

After a row, when couples have a postmortem, they pour over what was said and how they feel. The last thing they analyze is where the argument happened. Once when I got stuck with a couple and could not find a way to break through their bickering, I decided to take a different approach. I stopped asking what happened and asked where. The effect was miraculous. Instead of rehashing the issues, they took a step back and became more analytical. So I did some research with my other clients in order to discover where they argued and what the location said about their relationship.

## The Three Most Productive Places for Arguments

🌸 **1. CAR: It's not just backseat driving, traffic jams, and problems finding somewhere that makes the car the place you are most likely to have a row.** In our busy twenty-first-century lives, it is one of the few extended times that we spend with our partners. Unlike at home, it is hard to storm off when arguments get heated. Plus, with the driver's attention fixed on the road, we think a controversial issue might be easier to slip into general conversation. Certainly our partner will find it harder to spot if we are anxious, blushing, or being devious. However, without direct eye contact, our body language and intentions and more likely to be misunderstood.

**What it says about your relationship:** With a driver and a passenger, nowhere are the issues of control and power more out in the open. Arguments in the car are really about who is in charge. Modern couples like to feel they are equal, but underneath the surface one half often feels powerless.

**Solve it:** In successful relationships control is divided. For example, one will be in charge of money while the other organizes the social life. Draw up a list of activities, areas of the house, and responsibilities and put down who has the final say by each. If the balance is uneven, discuss which areas can be passed over. Always consult your partner in your areas and be careful not to belittle their opinions.

🍾 **2. KITCHEN: This is mission control in any house and the place that couples are most likely to meet at stressful times—like first thing in the morning.** The kitchen also throws up plenty of fuel for a row: unwashed dishes left lying around, clothes not taken out of the tumble dryer, or using the last of the milk. If you have children, it often provides somewhere to hiss at each other away from prying ears—while they are busy watching TV in the living room or finishing their homework in their bedrooms.

**What it says about your relationship:** Do you really feel appreciated? At the bottom of many domestic arguments one or both feel taken for granted. However, rather than focus on the causes, many couples unwittingly concentrate on the small surface issues and beat themselves up because they believe the rows are out of all proportion.

**Solve it:** Compliments and "thank yous" are really important. Nobody can ever have enough praise. When first courting, we leave each other notes and buy surprise bars of chocolate—don't stop just because the relationship is established. Next time you tell your partner you love her or him, add on one of the reasons why. It might seem like a joke— "because you make a great lasagna"—but it makes your love declaration seem less of a reflex and more grounded.

🍾 **3. OUT AND ABOUT: Many couples deliberately discuss controversial subjects in coffee shops and restaurants.** They feel it is harder to lose their tempers in public and hope witnesses will keep them both rational. Other couples row at parties after alcohol has loosened their tongues or because secretly they hope friends or family will take their side. Finally, shopping with your partner is another opportunity for conflict.

**What it says about your relationship:** In these relationships, an argument is often seen as a failure. You try to be rational and many times convince yourself there is really nothing major to be angry about—so why upset the apple cart? However, a lot of feelings are being repressed.

**Solve it:** Understand that rows are part of a healthy relationship. Letting off steam can be the first step to solving a dispute. If you are going out to discuss issues to be away from the kids, think again. Hearing their parents bring up issues and solve them is the best way for children to learn how to do it themselves.

## The Three Least Productive Places for Arguments

🌹 **1. LIVING ROOM: The television is often the focus in the living room and an ever-present excuse not to engage: "Could we talk about this later? I'm watching my program."** Although generally a pacifier, TV can occasionally be the source of conflict. If you're the jealous type, you might be tempted to monitor whether your partner is too interested in semiclothed actresses or actors. Plot lines can also spark submerged issues: "That's just the sort of thing you'd do."

**What it says about your relationship:** Are you depersonalizing any conflict, afraid that it will get out of hand? However, talking about issues second-hand—through the soap operas—takes the argument out of your hands into the scriptwriters'.

**Solve it:** Instead of backing up your case with other people's opinions—what your friends or family think—own the opinions: "I don't like it when you put your feet on the couch" rather than "My friend was disgusted when she saw you acting like a slob." This will stop your partner becoming quite so defensive and make him or her more likely to hear what you have to say.

🌱 **2. BEDROOM: Couples are more likely to kiss and make up in the bedroom than argue.** Although different levels of desire can cause tension, sex in general is such a difficult subject couples repress rather than talk over these issues. If the relationship is in real crisis, one partner will often go to bed earlier and pretend to be asleep when the other finally comes to bed.

**What it says about your relationship:** Arguing in the bedroom is a sure sign that you are overtired. Tension at bedtimes will make sleep more difficult and further exacerbate the problem. How good is your love life? Has an OK sex life drifted into something boring and unfulfilling?

**Solve it:** Look at your priorities. Are you taking on too much? How can you change your evenings to give more time to talk and solve problems. Don't be afraid to also set aside time for love making—so sex is no longer the last effort of an exhausted mind and body.

🌱 **3. BACKYARD AND GARDEN: It is not the soothing effect of nature that makes this the place couples are least likely to fight.** Arguing in public is embarrassing enough without having to face witnesses the next day and, unlike family, neighbors are particularly unforgiving and prone to gossiping.

**What it says about your relationship:** These arguments are out of control and a sign that a couple can't live together but can't let go. They promise that next time around everything will be better, but soon fall into the same old pattern.

**Solve it:** Agreeing to try harder is not enough. You need to step back and really understand what drives your arguments and why they have become so destructive.

## SUMMING UP

Every relationship has problems; it is how you deal with them that's important. Misunderstandings, problems, and rows are "six of one and half a dozen of the other"; by taking this on-board, couples will stop blaming each other. The second law of relationship disputes—emotional equals attract—shows that not only do both halves of a couple have equal skills to draw on to solve a row, but that these skills are normally complementary. If a dispute seems insoluble, look at how the eighty percent from the past is driving the twenty percent from today.

## IN A NUTSHELL:

- Take stock and understand what drives your arguments.

- Identify your good and unhelpful habits. What would you like to change?

- Find a middle way. Having no rows can be just as harmful as having too many.

# CHAPTER TWO

---

# Stop What Doesn't Work

**W**ouldn't it be wonderful if you could just ask nicely and your partner would go along with your request? Wouldn't life be much simpler if the two of you could agree the best course of action and get on with it rather than be bogged down in arguments, stonewalling, or procrastination. If this sounds like an impossible dream, don't worry because my love hacks will help you identify the sticking points, communicate better, and change your relationship for the better.

Up to now, you have probably tried a variety of ways to get your partner to change, but without much success. Common sense would suggest that, if they haven't worked, you should stop and try something else. Unfortunately, most people keep on with the same failed strategy, in the hope that doing it bigger, louder, or just one more time will provide the breakthrough. Sadly, they just dig themselves into a bigger hole. That's why the next love hack is to stop digging and throw away the spade.

## SEVEN FAILED STRATEGIES

None of these strategies are particularly effective—beyond the short term—but we keep on plugging away regardless. Which of the following have you used?

## Lecturing

**Definition:** Assuming the position of an expert or all-seeing prophet (who can foresee all the pitfalls) and telling your partner the errors of his or her ways—over and over again.

**In action:** "I wouldn't do it like that" or "You're not going to … ?" Although someone who lectures might think that they are being helpful, they really want to control their partner and ensure he or she performs the task their way.

"My wife believes there is only one way to change a diaper—with at least three baby wipes pulled out in advance and wiping down rather than up—and she has a real go if I don't follow her directions to the letter," explained Richard. At the same time, his wife, Caroline, would complain that he didn't help enough with the baby. "But you don't want help, you want staff to order about," Richard countered.

**How it backfires:** Assuming that you know best invites rebellion either overtly or covertly.

**What's the alternative?** Offer help and then step back; your partner will either learn from his or her mistakes or return and ask for advice. Richard soon discovered that some of his wife's directions were helpful and if, for example, he didn't fasten the straps properly then the diaper would sag. Caroline discovered she was much more relaxed, and enjoyed family time together, if she wasn't monitoring the amount of baby powder Richard used.

## Sarcasm

**Definition:** Using mocking or contemptuous put-downs, which are designed to control by making the other person feel small or stupid.

**In action:** This strategy goes hand-in-hand with sniping (hidden or sly undermining) and snapping with impatience. When Mason brought home an espresso coffee machine that one of his friends had bought but changed his mind about, he was upset that Kimberly didn't seem very grateful: "She was doing stuff online and beyond a cursory look didn't come down to give me a hand setting up the machine. It took some of the shine off the surprise—and she's the coffee drinker not me." So Mason shouted up the stairs: "If it's not too much trouble, could you come down and try this?"

**How it backfires:** Nobody likes criticism and most people fight back with similar ammunition. Indeed, Kimberly sniped back: "The milk isn't very frothy. Did you read the instructions?"

**What's the alternative?** However strong the temptation to respond to your partner's barbed comments, don't rise to the bait—but simply walk away. When your temper is more under control, explain how you feel and discuss the issues with your partner. When Mason and Kimberly both calmed down—after rowing all evening—Mason explained how he'd been looking forward to her reaction and Kimberly apologized.

## Demanding

**Definition:** Issuing commands rather than requests. If you use this strategy you do not expect to be told "no" or to be contradicted.

**In action:** This normally happens when someone feels in the right and therefore their partner is in the wrong (even though life is seldom this black and white). When Siobhan discovered that her husband, Declan, had had an affair, she demanded that he take her away for a second honeymoon: "You've spent enough on that woman, you can spend a little on me." However, she was so busy imposing her will on Declan that she was unable to hear his concerns: "How is going away going to change things between us?" Rather than answering his question, Siobhan just restated her case but this time with tears: "He's broken my heart but he won't even do this little thing for me."

**How it backfires:** Although people may give into demands, they subvert in sneaky ways, such as finding millions of excuses for never quite getting around to the task. Alternatively, like Declan, they just dig their heels in and refuse to budge—even an inch—fearing that their partner will steamroller them into submission.

**What's the alternative?** Negotiating. In this way, your partner is allowed to express her or his opinions—which may or may not be valid—discuss the time scale for a project and take joint ownership of a project. When Declan and Siobhan finished counseling, and resolved the underlying problems in their marriage, they did indeed choose and plan a weekend away together.

## Nagging

**Definition:** The first time is asking, the second time reminding, but further repetition becomes nagging.

**In action:** Nothing polarizes a couple quicker than nagging. The person being nagged feels their partner is always finding fault (and therefore feels hard done by), while the person nagging—and it's something of which both men and women are guilty—feels powerless and angry.

"If she doesn't like being nagged, she could put her shoes away," says James, twenty-eight, "but she kicks them off and leaves them for me to trip over. I've tried asking, I've tried explaining that I could easily damage them, I've tried throwing them over to her side of the bedroom. I'll talk until I'm blue in the face and although she might remember for a few days, nothing really changes." Although James thought he'd been trying lots of different ways of communicating, he'd actually just been nagging. Unfortunately, his girlfriend, Michelle, just switched off. Worse still, she used his "unreasonable" nagging to justify carrying on as before.

**How it backfires:** Nobody likes to nag and nobody likes to be nagged. It creates a slow poison that seeps through a relationship.

**What's the alternative? Bring all the hostility up to the surface by asking:** "How can we resolve this problem?" Be prepared to listen to your partner's viewpoint and this will encourage him or her to listen to yours. James explained that he felt taken for granted—and not appreciated for what he did around the house—and Michelle explained what it felt like to be hounded. They were finally ready to cooperate.

## Inducing Guilt

**Definition:** Manipulating a partner by making him or her feel responsible for your upset or by convincing them that they have committed an offense.

**In action:** It normally starts with a prod to get sympathy or pity: "I never see my children" or "my life is a mess," and if someone else has a bad day it's "not as bad as mine"—but this strategy is really a request for a free pass to get your own way. The next step up reminds your partner how much he or she is in debt: "After everything I've done for you" or "I don't like washing your gym clothes." However, there is a more sinister twist. "My girlfriend and I were at the grocery store and I ran into an old friend who is almost like a sister to me," explains Jake, twenty-nine. "She helped me through a bad patch and I did a lot of babysitting for her when her husband left. I hadn't seen her for a while so stopped and chatted. I could tell my girlfriend was getting more and more annoyed, so I made my apologies and got on with the shopping. Immediately, my girlfriend started having a go about how inconsiderate I'd been and how I'd ignored her—even though I'd introduced her and tried to involve her in our conversation. 'I was disrespectful. I didn't consider her feelings. I had no boundaries.' To be honest, I didn't really understand but I apologized for upsetting her—except it didn't make any difference. She was in such a mood that she drove away from the grocery store without looking and almost crashed into another car—that was my fault too." In effect, Jake's girlfriend was taking a minor or imaginary offense, winding herself up over it, and then blaming Jake for upsetting her.

**How it backfires:** Although this strategy will often get the desired effect, any victory feels hollow as nothing is freely given by their partner and the guilt inducer, who already suffers from low-esteem, feels even more worthless.

**What's the alternative?** Instead of blaming your partner, and therefore giving her or him all the power to remedy the situation, look at your own part in the problem. It is not only easier to change your behavior than force change on to your partner, but taking control is empowering.

## Placating

**Definition:** Trying to appease, sweet talk, and pacify your partner and thereby take the edge off his or her bad mood.

**In action:** Martha and Greg had been married for fifteen years, but for much of that time Greg had suffered from depression. "Obviously, I've tried to be supportive and understanding," said Martha, "but sometimes I think I've spent my whole life tiptoeing around him, monitoring his mood, and trying to keep everything nice. I know I want to grow old with him but not this gloomy, insecure, sleeping all weekend version of him. But I don't say any of this because I'm worried about making him feel worse." Unfortunately, she had built up a head of resentment: "What about me? It would be good not to be taken for granted."

**How it backfires:** Whether you are using smiles (that are put on), too-ready agreement, or forced humor, you are still trying to control. Worse still, this strategy often makes the other person even more annoyed.

**What's the alternative?** It is much better to address the issues—however unpleasant—rather than sidestep a row.

## Dropping Hints

**Definition:** Hoping your partner will guess or know what is needed, rather asking outright for it.

**In action:** Sometimes this strategy can be quite aggressive—"If you loved me you'd know"—but generally it comes from a position of weakness. Martha certainly didn't expect anyone to be interested in her needs, so even if she felt down and wanted a hug she wouldn't say anything: "I've always got my satisfaction from looking after other people; the children and Greg have always come first."

"What would happen if you did ask?" I inquired.

Martha was silent for a while: "If you don't really ask, then you don't have to deal with the rejection when you don't get."

**How it backfires:** Clues can be misinterpreted and hints can be so subtle that they are missed altogether.

**What's the alternative?** Value yourself and accept that it is OK to have needs and to express them.

## WHY DO I ADOPT THIS STRATEGY?

One of the best ways of breaking out of unhelpful behavior is identifying why you do it.

🌱 **1. Understand the roots.** Our first experiences of trying to get our own way come when we are only two or three years old. Our language skills are not very well developed and we are too young to understand concepts like negotiation or compromise. Worse still, our parents hold all the cards. It is not surprising that we learn as children to wheedle, demand, or throw tantrums. In many ways, the seven failed strategies are more sophisticated versions of toddler behavior.

🌱 **2. Understand the patterns.** We discover how relationships work from watching our parents and siblings interact. How would your mother get her way? How would your father impose his will? What would your brothers and sisters do? Who was in charge? How did they maintain their top-dog status? What are the links between how your family behaved and how you try to influence your partner?

🐾 **3. Understand the danger points.** Look back at the last three times you had a row or were left frustrated at not being able to influence your partner's behavior. What were the common themes? Were you tired or stressed? Had problems from work seeped into your personal life? Were you feeling unappreciated and therefore particularly vulnerable? By knowing the signs, you can be extra vigilant next time and think twice before behaving in the same old way.

# THE THREE KEYS TO SUCCESSFUL PERSUASION

Once you have stopped wasting energy and good-will on strategies that do not work, there is space to look at what does.

## 1. Equality

The failed strategies have one thing in common: a power imbalance. In the first three, the more powerful partner tries to bludgeon the other into submission and in the last three, the less powerful partner tries to manipulate the more powerful one. (With nagging, there is a twisted version of equality as two matched partners try to force and resist each other.) So what's the alternative? In true equality, as opposed to nagging, there is a benefit for each partner from the solution. Sometimes each partner has separate spheres of control—for example, one will be in charge of money, the other in charge of their social life—but each will consult the other and major decisions are made jointly. All in all, each partner will control about fifty percent of their life together.

Mason and Kimberly, who we met earlier in the chapter, arrived in counseling in crisis. Their fights were so destructive that even a minor disagreement would spiral out of control and ruin their whole week.

A typical example was when Mason came home and found Kimberly cleaning the saucepan they used to cook their pet rats' food. "She was about to tip the soapy water all over the garden. I asked her to stop because it would ruin the plants," said Mason, "but she just looked at me and poured it anyway." He had hardly finished explaining when Kimberly jumped in: "You didn't ask, you shouted. If you'd stopped and asked, I'd have told you that it wasn't soapy water but the last rinse." Mason gave her a black look and went straight back on the attack: "So why not put it down the drain?" Kimberly was so angry I thought she was about to walk out of my counseling room: "How could I with all your junk lying around?" They both felt the problem was the other's unreasonable behavior and if only he or she would change everything would be fine.

When we looked back at this argument, toward the end of their counseling, they were not only able laugh but identify that the breakthrough had been when both of them started changing—equally. "When I didn't lose my temper, Mason didn't close in on himself and shut me out," said Kimberly. "When I didn't retreat and keep my feelings and thoughts to myself, Kimberly stopped blowing her top," said Mason.

## 2. Put Yourself in Your Partner's Shoes

From where we stand, our solution makes complete sense. We understand the thought process that helped us reach this conclusion. If our preferred option seems a little one-sided, there is a good reason or a good excuse. Meanwhile, our partner has been through a parallel process—but while we expect her or him to listen to us, we are not quite so ready to offer the same courtesy. All too often, we half listen, throw in a bit of our own interpretation, and jump to the wrong conclusion. So while we put our actions down to the best possible motives, we can easily put our partner's down to the worst ones. But what would happen if you understood your partner's position as well as your own?

When Mason and Kimberly stopped countering each other's arguments and started listening or asking for further explanation, they began to understand each other better. "We both came from families where nobody listened to us," said Kimberly. "And instead of making assumptions—often the wrong ones—we've started to check it out first," added Mason.

## 3. Win/Win Solutions

When you and your partner see each other as adversaries, the goal is outright victory or to win concessions. Therefore, the strategy becomes to dig into your position, mislead, or use tricks to get your own way. The result is either a Win/Lose situation where only one side sees the outcome as positive (and the other is less likely to accept the solution voluntarily) or a Lose/Lose situation where both parties end up worse off.

The alternative is a Win/Win solution where both parties benefit and therefore the solutions stick. So how do you achieve this goal? The secret is to understand that behind every bargaining position there are not only needs and desires but concerns and fears too. Our natural inclination is to close down debate, as we fear that the more competing interests come to the surface, the harder it will be to find a solution. However, Win/Win depends on identifying as many interests as possible. In fact, the more we know about both our own true needs and those of our partner, the easier it becomes to find a solution that benefits everyone.

With the focus on interests—rather than positions—and by considering multiple criteria rather than looking for one answer, we can begin to use reason and yield to principles rather than pressure. This process not only reduces our fears, but once all the needs are in the open it is easier to help each other. Before too long, we have become a team, rather than adversaries, and a Win/Win solution is almost inevitable. So how does it work in practice?

When Mason and Kimberly discussed their finances—each had a separate bank account—they shared their needs, desires, concerns, and fears. Their need was to find a simpler way to run their household accounts rather than forever debating whose turn it was to pay. Kimberly desired a joint account, so she did not feel like a small girl asking Daddy for money. Mason's concern was that the bills got paid on time. "I'm not frightened that she will blow the budget—although I've had girlfriends before who were hopeless with money—because she's really quite good with finances," he said. "Actually, my job involves keeping an eye on costs," Kimberly added. So they decided to keep their individual accounts but to set up a joint one for household bills. It was a classic Win/Win solution. Kimberly became more involved in their finances. Mason had some of the pressure of balancing the budget taken off him.

## Turn it Around

Next time a contentious issue comes up between you are your partner, put it to this test:

- **Do I really want it?** Sometimes being denied something or your partner telling you what to do can put your back up and launch a fight. Instead of acting on automatic pilot, stop and check this is something you truly want rather than something you just think you want.

- **Is it really fair?** What would an independent arbitrator say? Do you have a reasonable case? If you stripped away all your self-justifications—probably drawn from a different part of your life—how fair is this particular request?

- **Is it really important?** Lots of bitter arguments are over matters of principle rather than over a particular issue. When the matters of principle are removed, arguments such as Mason and Kimberly's over how to clean the rats' saucepan are neither that contentious nor worth the amount of upset caused.

- **Think past the moment.** Although using one of your old strategies to win an advantage might feel good, think past your moment of triumph to the mood in the house over the next few days and then on to the impact on your relationship.

## SUMMING UP

We think that we've used a variety of strategies to gain our partner's cooperation but really we've used the same failed ones over and over again. These include lecturing, sarcasm, and being demanding (trying to be more powerful than your partner) or inducing guilt, placating, and dropping hints (imagining your partner has all the power). The other strategy is nagging, which sets up a classic Lose/Lose situation where nothing is achieved and both parties feel powerless. The alternative is to place yourself in your partner's shoes, look for solutions that are equal, and allow both of you to win.

## IN A NUTSHELL:

- When you stop trying to force change, your partner will stop resisting change.

- Good-will can return to your relationship.

- Your partner is finally open to being persuaded.

# CHAPTER THREE

---

# Do Less

**W**henever long-married couples are asked the secret of their success, they invariably reply: you have to work at things. But shouldn't our relationships be a source of joy rather than something to knuckle down under? The other problem with working on a relationship is that it suggests making big changes—like setting up a weekly date night, going on a second honeymoon, or making big sacrifices (for example, giving up a friend who your partner dislikes or cutting back on a hobby that eats into family time.)

Over thirty years' experience as a marital therapist has shown me that these big changes seldom deliver the big benefits that couples desire. Date night might work a few times but problems getting babysitters soon undermine good intentions, the glow of the second honeymoon quickly wears off, and people soon resent their sacrifices. Worse still, when the big effort changes very little, couples begin to believe their relationship is doomed.

So if "working" on your relationship can so easily backfire, what about the other extreme: doing nothing? With this strategy, however, there's a real danger of slipping into taking each other for granted and nobody wants that either.

Fortunately, I have another love hack to provide a middle way ...

# THE LAZY GUIDE TO WORKING ON YOUR RELATIONSHIP

All these ideas are fun, simple, and don't take much effort. However, taken together, they can overhaul your relationship and turn time together from dull into desirable:

## Ten Minutes Chatting Over Your Day

Instead of big dramatic gestures—which are hard to repeat—try to set up good relationship habits. The most important one is checking in with each other when you return home—instead of, for example, starting supper or checking emails. A few moments sharing the highs and the lows of the day prevents misunderstandings—such as your partner's bad mood is down to you rather than his or her demanding boss—which can ruin a whole evening together. The more details in your daily chat, the more involved you become in each other's triumphs and disasters. Some couples find it hard to share—after years of broad brushstrokes of "fine" or "same old thing." So remember small anecdotes and snippets of gossip about friends and save them up for the evening. A good tip is to sit down and eat together—without the television on—as this gives enough time together for the natural rhythms of conversation to kick in.

## Watch Each Other's Favorite Television Show

Instead of catching up on chores, watching another channel in a different room, or going online, commit to sitting through each other's must-see show. This will provide something new to discuss and demonstrate that you are truly interested in each other—even the inconvenient bits, such as an obsession with axle grease or a passion for fashion. What's more, we have a real animal need to be close to another human being and snuggling up together on the couch is not only a good way to unwind but also shows that you can be intimate without it necessarily leading to sex.

## Kiss With Your Eyes Open

Actually looking at each other when you kiss is incredibly intimate and can also be the gateway to more erotic lovemaking. Perhaps that's why this is the most controversial of my ideas. Some couples find the idea silly or feel uncomfortable looking at each other. They believe it is more "romantic" to keep their eyes closed, but this makes us concentrate on the sensation rather the person.

When couples arrive in my office with one partner complaining "you're not the person I thought you were," I can almost guarantee that they have been kissing with their eyes closed and getting lost in their own fantasies. So persevere, overcome the awkwardness, and become more aware of both your partner and yourself and take lovemaking to a whole new level.

Another associated idea is to mix up your kissing style, try butterfly kisses (very light and not just on the mouth but all over your partner's face), nibbling kisses (gentle bites on the lips or other sensual areas like the ears), or breathy languid kisses, tasting and smelling each other's body.

## Buy Something Small But Fun

It could be her favorite bar of chocolate or a novelty key ring for him, but a present shows that you're thinking about your partner even when apart. Unlike birthdays and Christmas when it is tempting to buy presents your partner "needs"—such as clothes you think make her look sexy or tools for jobs you'd like him to do around the house—these gifts are pure fun or indulgence. There is a second advantage: by modeling the sort of spontaneous appreciation that you'd like—where flowers are not just for birthdays but "because I saw these and thought of you" and saying "thank you" is not just for completing a major project but everyday chores too—you are encouraging your partner to adopt the same behavior.

## Share a Bath

There are few better ways of unwinding after a long hard day than a soak in the bath, but instead of making it a solitary pursuit invite your partner along. I counseled one couple who bathed together every day—as somewhere to talk without the kids interrupting. A twist on this idea is bringing along a large bowl of ice cream and one spoon. It is very sensual to feed each other something cold in a hot bath. Sharing a bath, and washing each other's hair, will also help you and your partner to feel comfortable being naked together and improves overall intimacy.

## Go to Bed at the Same Time or Enjoy a Sleep-In Together

If you and your partner's body clocks are on different time zones, and you're seldom awake in bed together, the chances of making love are close to zero. So make a conscious choice to communicate better over bedtimes. Instead of saying "I'm going to bed now" and hoping that your partner will follow, invite him or her. Instead of watching any old garbage on television until you're tired enough to sleep, come upstairs for a cuddle and drift off in each other's arms. Skip jobs, such as loading the washing machine or checking emails, before going upstairs or you'll miss the window when your partner is still awake. If you have radically different bedtimes, try finding a compromise where, for example, your partner goes up a little earlier and you stay up a little longer and meet in the middle. Conversely, give yourself a treat, let the children look after themselves next Sunday morning, and enjoy a sleep-in together.

## Give In With Good Grace

Living with someone inevitably means having to compromise and do things that you'd rather not. Next time you have to attend her miserable work's do or hold a piece of wood that he's sawing through, don't just grit your teeth but look for the hidden pleasures. Even if you have

DO LESS

you have to "act as if" you're enjoying yourself, after a while you will probably start to believe it. Not only will your partner be grateful but he or she will go the extra mile for you in return.

## Look at Each Other More

When they're talking, couples in love spend 75 percent of their time looking at each other. Most settled couples are too busy buttoning up their children's coats or buttering sandwiches to make eye contact— even when communicating something important. In fact, they only look at each for 30 to 60 percent of the time and therefore miss the subtleties of body language and misinterpret each other's tone of voice.

While good eye contact makes you seem attentive and sincere, poor eye contact makes your partner think you are talking at them rather than to them. So at the very least, make a commitment to be in the same room rather than shouting up the stairs.

## Report Your Negative Feelings Rather Than Show Them

In today's United States, we are forever being told to express our feelings. However, when it comes to anger, getting things off your chest can often pump up your emotions rather than reduce them. Worse still, having a rant will either encourage your partner to fight back— and escalate matters further—or to sulk, switch off, or walk away (which means nothing ever gets sorted). So instead of showing your feelings, try reporting them instead. By this I mean: "I felt angry when you didn't answer me" or "I was disappointed when you were late," rather than snapping, sniping, or shouting. Your partner will probably apologize or offer an explanation and the two of you can have a civilized discussion about how to do things differently.

## Echo Each Other

This is the simplest and most effective way of improving communication. When your partner's finished telling you something, repeat

43

back the last thing said. For example: "So you just stood there." This might seem weird, but it shows your partner that she or he has your full attention. It is also encourages her or him to open up and tell you more. The final benefit of echoing back is that it takes the pressure off you to think up a searching question. Although this strategy might feel a little artificial at first, persevere and it will soon become second nature.

## EXERCISE   HOW GOOD A LISTENER ARE YOU?

When we don't understand our partner's behavior, we imagine that we need to ask clever or searching questions, but the truth is our partner is telling us all we need to know in their everyday conversation. The problem is that much of the time we are not listening. The following quiz tests if you are good listener or not:

1. When your partner is having trouble finding the words to express him or herself, what are you most likely to do?

    a) Finish off his or her sentence.

    b) Nod encouragingly.

2. When your partner needs help with a problem at work what is most likely to happen?

    a) I will offer advice or come up with a way forward.

    b) I will ask for more information, so that I really understand the situation, and check all possible avenues are explored.

3. How often does your partner complain that you interrupt?

    a) Quite often he or she will say, "If you'll just let me finish."

    b) We generally hear each other out.

**4.** When your partner is recounting a story about something that happened during the day, which of the following are you most likely to be doing?

   a) Going through a difficult problem at work, keeping an eye on the children, or ticking off which jobs have been done and noting those still to do.

   b) Picturing what your partner is talking about or making encouraging noises such as "yes," "really," or "tell me more."

**5.** When your partner is moaning or complaining about something you've done what are you thinking about?

   a) Ways to refute the complaint or about his or her equally irritating failings.

   b) Does he or she have a fair case?

**6.** Which of the following do you naturally prefer?

   a) Talking.

   b) Listening.

**Mostly a):** Although you hear what is being said to you—and can repeat chunks of information back—you are not really listening. There are probably tapes playing in your brain and other forms of intrusive thinking that are stopping you from paying your partner the level of attention that you'd like yourself. Next time your mind wanders, mentally push the thought out of your head—you can attend to it later—and concentrate on what is being said.

**Mostly b):** Congratulations. You are a good listener. However, look back at the areas where you answered a) rather than b). Actively listening—i.e., asking questions and really trying to understand your partner without jumping to conclusions—is really difficult. How could you improve?

# THINK SMALL

Change is unsettling. It makes us anxious and frightened. Worse still, we are programmed to respond to fear in one of two ways: fight or flight. But don't worry, there's a way around this problem. It's called Kaizen, from the Japanese for "change" (*kai*) and "good" (*zen*), and stresses the importance of continuous improvement. Instead of trying for big changes, Kaizen aims to bypass our fears and our natural inclination to stick with the familiar by taking small steps.

In a famous study, southern Californian householders were asked to put up a small "Be a safe driver" sign in their windows. Most people agreed. Two weeks later, the team returned and this time asked the volunteers to put up a huge sign—bearing the same message—on their front lawns. They were shown pictures, so there could be no mistake that these signs would dwarf their homes. To make the billboards even less attractive, the lettering was poorly executed. At the same time, the team visited another neighborhood, which matched the profile of the first but where the residents had not previously agreed to take the small sign. Not surprisingly, only 17 percent of these householders agreed to display the safe driver billboard. In contrast, 76 percent of the homes with a small sign opted for the large sign. The small step had made them four times as likely to take the big step.

When couples are stuck and unable to find a way forward, I find Kaizen can break the deadlock. This is how it can work for you:

## Ask Small Questions

Our brain actually likes small questions; this is why we do quizzes and puzzles or enjoy explaining to friends the best way to cook a turkey. We feel good when we know the answer and, with little at stake, don't feel a fool if we get something wrong.

Jane and Christopher, in their late thirties, had a big problem. He was fed up with his work, bored with everyday life, and felt all the passion had drained out of their relationship: "We have nothing whatsoever in common. When I have free time, I'd much rather be out hunting deer than at home with Jane. Surely, that's wrong." He hadn't quite gone as far as saying he didn't love her anymore but Jane worried that their relationship had no future. "I wish I hadn't told you and just pretended that everything was OK," said Christopher. Jane countered: "What good is that going to do? We've got to get this sorted out. I can't hang around waiting for you to decide if you want me or not." Before arriving in counseling, they had used only big solutions and Jane had asked Christopher to sleep at his parents' for a week.

"What did that achieve, beyond making me get up earlier and get even more tired?" he complained.

"I thought it would give you space to think," said Jane.

"By the time we'd put the children to bed and I'd driven around to their house, I had enough time to make a cup of coffee and go to bed."

Using the Kaizen way, I didn't ask big questions like: Why do you feel this way? (As Christopher would have probably answered: "I don't know. If I knew do you think I'd be putting myself through all this?") Instead, I asked the couple to consider: "What one small step could I take toward improving your relationship?" and "What one special thing about you and your partner could you build on?"

**Warning:** Frame your question as a positive. Instead of: "Why don't you fancy me?" Turn it into: "How could we improve our sex life?"

## Solve Small Problems

Many people find it hard to think of any small problems in their relationship, especially when the large ones are staring them in the face. However, it is just these minor irritations that slowly undermine our relationship. By ignoring small problems—because we're too busy with day-to-day life or it doesn't seem worth rocking the boat—we redefine them as "normal" and lose sight of them altogether.

So if you're unable to come up with any small problems, close your eyes and picture what happens on a normal day between you and your partner—moment by moment. Start with getting up in the morning and end with going to bed. Every time there is something that makes you wince—however small—stop your imaginary movie and write down the "normal" problem. Before too long, you will have a list of small issues to consider.

When Jane did this exercise during a solo session, she stopped in the middle of describing preparing breakfast for the children. (Christopher had a long commute but would get up at the last minute and hardly have enough to time to drink a coffee.) "From time to time, he'll complain that I haven't put on the coffee machine and he's got to drink instant, but he doesn't understand that Lola is a fussy eater and Jack won't sit at the table. I've got my hands full. If he cares that much, get up five minutes earlier."

"What message does that give Christopher?" I asked.

Jane thought for a while. "I put the children first."

A small problem—making coffee in the morning—had been categorized as "normal" and therefore ignored. So instead of trying to deal with big issues—like bringing back the passion into their relationship—Jane made a pot of fresh coffee in the morning. At their next joint session, their mood had lightened. We still had a long way to go but the sense of being stuck—that nothing could ever change—had gone.

**Warning:** Be specific as possible about the problem. Don't go for global issues such as "Show some respect" or "Help more around the house" but make them specific: "Don't interrupt me when I'm trying to tell you something" or "Transfer the clothes from the washing machine to the dryer when you get home."

## Take Small Steps

Small questions throw the spotlight on small problems, which need to be solved by small steps. It is also helpful if you can find something that comes up fairly often, so you can check your progress. Kaizen also works best when the solutions can be implemented straightaway.

As their counseling progressed, Jane began to agree with Christopher's diagnosis of their relationship: "He's right. We don't do enough together. Before the kids were born, and we were dating, I'd go off with him on their hunting expeditions but after a while there seemed better things to do." So she decided to ask her mother to take the children one Sunday and, as an experiment, go with Christopher to one of his hunts. "I told myself to have an open mind—because it can be cold and boring—but I found myself really enjoying it. There had been a light dusting of snow and the countryside looked wonderful. I was out in the fresh air and it was really nice watching Christopher. There were other wives to talk to and afterward we had lunch altogether."

Christopher was equally pleased: "It was great to be able to share with you."

"And you touched my knee—by the fire."

"It felt right."

Jane was not going to attend every hunt but they had taken a small step in the right direction.

**Warning:** Double-check that the changes are truly small. If your goal is, for example, improving your diet, giving up chocolate might seem a small step but actually it could be hard to follow through. However, if your small step was to throw away the first square of every bar, this would be reasonably easy. Over the coming weeks, you could throw away more and more chocolate. Next, you could leave half of your dessert in a restaurant and so on.

The Kaizen way stresses that it is better to build on a small success than make a big gesture that is likely to fail. If you're looking for inspiration for a small step to change your relationship, try the following exercise.

## REMEMBERING THE MAGIC OF THE FIRST MEETING

For five years, I did a series of magazine profiles of celebrities and their partners. I would always start by asking for the story of how the couple first met. Within seconds the atmosphere in the room would change–any nerves or apprehension would disappear–and I would feel real warmth as people remembered. The secret is in the detail I asked for: Where were you? What were you wearing? What did you eat? What did your partner look like? What did she say? What did he do? Normally people have boiled down their "how we met" story into one or two sentences, but this reflex story does not provide enough material to trigger proper memories. Over and over again, the celebrities–normally on tight time schedules–would stretch the time allocated for my interview. I was taking them back to the magic of their first meeting and everybody enjoyed lingering on these passionate memories a while longer.

Either write a short story about your memories of how you met your partner or bring the topic up in general conversation–perhaps over a meal. It normally takes three or four questions to get someone in the mood. To give you an idea, here is the first part of my interview with Twiggy (sixties model and star of the film *The Boyfriend*) and her husband Leigh Lawson (an actor best known for his roles as Alec D'Uberville in Polanski's film *Tess*). See how many facts I extracted.

Twiggy started: "In 1985, I went out for dinner at Caprice in London with three friends. At another table I spotted the actor Jonathan Pryce–who I'd been working with–so I went over to say hello. Immediately this handsome man stood up. It was Leigh, who reminded me that we'd met ten years earlier at a John Denver concert. Even back then I'd thought him really attractive, but we'd both been married then so nothing romantic crossed my mind. This time the chemistry must have been obvious because I remember telling my friends to stop trying to pair me off. But I must have been curious because I bought a magazine with a big interview with Leigh. I learned he had been alone for two years and after the trauma of the breakup was not interested in seeing anyone seriously for the next ten years! Three days later some friends invited me to a restaurant in Chelsea. By a string of amazing coincidences, Leigh was invited too. We chatted and laughed but on paper he was trouble. Who in their right mind would trust a gorgeous actor? I was no longer an eighteen year old about to jump in headfirst. So I let him slip away again. Fate had other ideas."

At this point, Leigh takes up the story: "I thought Twiggy was absolutely gorgeous—but as she was one of the most beautiful woman in the world I knew everybody would be after her phone number. Despite fate throwing the two of us into the same restaurant twice in one week, I said goodnight and let her walk away. Perhaps I lacked confidence; perhaps my heart had just got out of intensive care; perhaps she wasn't giving the green light—although these days Twigs claims she was disappointed that I didn't ask for her number, but she's got to say that! Anyway, five days later I went to the newsagents for my morning paper and this big blue Jaguar—with an exquisite blonde inside—pulled up by the curb. It was Twiggy. She wound down the window and said: 'Do you want a cup of tea?' Even I knew this was the green light!"

Every story of how two people met and fell in love is interesting, so give yourself permission to enjoy your own. With luck, there will be things to tease each other about (notice how Leigh does it over asking for the telephone number and Twiggy over the magazine interview) which in turn can be turned into general affectionate everyday banter between the two of you. How did the two of you meet? What coincidences brought the two of you together? Do you tease each other about these events?

## START ASKING IN A CLEAR AND EFFECTIVE WAY

Once the atmosphere between you and your partner has improved, you can try a small step toward better cooperation by asking for something directly. Although this might be a risky step, your chances of success are greater than you imagine.

Francis Flynn is the Associate Professor of Organizational Behavior at Stanford University in California; she did three studies where people were asked to estimate the likelihood that others would agree to a direct request for help. These included asking strangers to borrow a cell phone, to escort them to a specific nearby destination, and to make donations to a charity. She discovered that we underestimate our chances of success by a staggering 50 percent.

The following tips will help boost the likelihood of getting a pleasant surprise to your request for help:

🌺 **1. Make it something small.** Remember, the aim is to tiptoe past your partner's fears.

🌺 **2. Keep the stakes low.** For the first request, make it simple: Could you pass me the newspaper? Could you cut some mint from the backyard for me? Avoid something that you want desperately and would be upset about if your partner refused.

🌺 **3. Double-check.** Is it a fair request? Is it easy for my partner to achieve?

🌺 **4. Choose your time.** If your partner is about to rush out the door or is deep into some task, he or she will be less likely to stop and help. So don't sabotage the request before you've even begun by asking at the wrong moment.

🌺 **5. Don't dress it up.** Forget the preambles like "I don't often ask but ..." or "I know you're busy but ..." or give explanations about why you need help: "I'm really behind with this recipe and you know they're always early ..." The danger is that your partner will have switched off before the request, have heard the preamble as an attack, or been unwittingly handed an excuse for not cooperating. So keep it simple: "Please could you ...?"

🌺 **6. Be prepared to try again.** Persuasive people don't let one mishap stop them. It often takes one or two attempts to ask in a clear and effective way.

## SUMMING UP

When we are unhappy, we think the answer is to make big changes. Unfortunately, this sort of revolution is frightening for our partners who will either fight back or bury themselves in work, hobbies, and looking after the children. Many people think the only alternative is to do nothing, but this leads to a feeling of hopelessness—fatal in the long term—or resentment. The answer, however, is to find a middle way: do less. Small steps allow a relationship to evolve and grow because they are nonthreatening and therefore bypass our natural fear of change.

## IN A NUTSHELL:

- If a journey of a thousand miles must begin with the first step, what small step could you make toward changing your relationship?

- Slow change is better than no change at all.

- Be interested in the small details of your partner's life and create a positive atmosphere where trust can flourish.

# CHAPTER FOUR

# Low-Conflict Relationships

No nasty rows, no falling out, and no bitterness—it sounds wonderful, but is it really possible to transcend any tensions and live blissfully ever after? In reality, arguing is an important part of a healthy partnership; it uncovers the issues that really matter and enables partners to distinguish between minor irritations and serious problems. An argument creates the impetus to speak out, cuts through excuses, and finally creates a sense that "something must be done." Although rows sometimes make us uncomfortable, sometimes that can be good.

So why are some people afraid to let rip with their loved ones? The first reason for being less confrontational is the trend for couples to be each other's best friend as well as lover. It's considered bad form for friends to scream at each other; friends should be supportive, understanding, and, most importantly, accept us as we are. "My husband has a terrible habit of interrupting people," says Savannah, a thirty-two-year-old market researcher. "His best man even joked about it in his wedding speech. I've tried teasing him but he says I knew his failings when I married him. So now I have to bite my lip."

Couples with children can be especially nervous of having rows. "Not in front of the children" is the buzzword for a generation that is ultra-cautious about undermining their sons' and daughters' confidence or causing other psychological problems. And, with children being allowed to stay up later as they get older, "not in front of the children" is soon transformed into seldom arguing at all. This is a pity because when children witness a constructive argument they learn important lessons about honesty, compromise, and reconciliation.

Another reason is that couples are simply too nice to argue. In many of these partnerships, one or both halves have watched their parents get divorced and are only too aware how apocalyptic a row can be. "The day we got married, I told Jim: 'I'll discuss, I'll listen, but I won't fight,'" says Lydia, a fifty-nine-year-old dental technician. "I watched my father and mother fight incessantly, and it's no way to live." In an insecure world, where work is forever restructured and our extended families live further apart, our relationships are more important than ever. Therefore, is it any wonder that we play safe and avoid the conflict?

Busy work schedules mean that couples spend less time together. On the most simplistic level, if you hardly see each other you have fewer opportunities to fight. But it goes deeper. Just as overworked parents stress the importance of "quality time" with their children, couples want what little time they do spend together to be perfect. Not only does this expectation put pressure on a couple to get the most out of their shared leisure time, but it also makes them less inclined to express their dissatisfaction. "Our only concentrated time together is on vacation or weekends away," explains Savannah's partner Robert, a thirty-five-year-old software salesman. "After splashing out thousands to fly to Europe, I was not going to let myself get jealous about the way Savannah flirted with the staff." It takes sustained time together to feel relaxed enough to let down your barriers and be open about your grievances. When does a two-career couple have that?

The changing nature of the workplace is another culprit in making us less likely to argue. New management techniques have done away with old-fashioned confrontation in favor of finding consensus, and this is making itself felt at home as well as in the office. Michael is a forty-year-old office manager whose wife, Sue, noticed a marked difference after a particular training course. "He decided we could only make a point if we were holding the talking stick—a wooden spoon from the kitchen," she explains. "I wanted to clock him with it. But every time I lost my temper he would calmly say things like 'I hear your anger' and "We won't get closure this way.' I had to keep telling him 'I'm not one of your middle managers.'" As Sue discovered, it takes two to make an argument.

Some younger high-flying couples—particularly those in their twenties—feel an immense pressure to be perfect. These individuals may have excelled in school, attended the best universities and colleges, graduated into exciting or high-paid jobs, and are now buying their own homes. The perfect relationship is another box to tick and, sadly, arguments do not fit into that profile. Harper, a twenty-seven-year-old TV researcher, speaks for many who strive for perfection: "I would have been mortified if any of our friends had known that Claude and I were having relationship problems." Harper was very concerned about achieving and worried if any of her contemporaries were promoted in case she was falling behind—and her marriage had become part of this competition. Unfortunately, this couple had played the game so well that even Harper was not aware of any serious difficulties until her husband disappeared for two months and reappeared on the other side of the world.

Other couples do not argue because one half is so keen to help the other grow that they almost become their personal therapist or guru. How can you complain about that? After all, it is done out of the best possible motive: "I just want the best for you." However, these well-intentioned partners can soon be telling their other halves how to feel. Logan, a forty-two-year-old financial consultant found himself in this position: "My father had died and I was in shock. I thought he'd always be there for me. How could this have happened?" I just wanted to sit quietly in the car and get my head straight. However, all the way through the four-hour car journey home, my wife kept on at me: 'You've got to get this out.'" There is a short step from trying to help someone to controlling them.

However, underlying all the above reasons for not arguing is one unifying fear: What will happen if a row gets out of control? My clients confess: "Often I'd like to get angry but I'm frightened I'll never stop," or "If I let it out, will I go completely nuts?" and "Will he think less of me?" or "What if she rejects me?" Of course, these are all perfectly reasonable concerns—especially for someone who has seldom let go before. Another group of couples have argued in the past but have had bad experiences: "When she loses her temper she shouts me down and I hate it" or "If I get angry he blanks me for days afterward and the atmosphere is horrible."

## TOP TEN TOPICS COUPLES ARGUE ABOUT

Over the past five years, I have been keeping a tally of what sparks rows. If you are in a low-conflict relationship, it is particularly helpful to know what provokes other people. How many of these issues sound familiar?

1. **Phone.** Not just how much time is spent looking at it—for work or pleasure—but developing special "friendships" and watching pornography.

2. **Time.** Always in short supply. No wonder we often complain that our partner hasn't got enough for us.

3. **Feeling Appreciated.** When we're tired, we take each other for granted. Also we're far more likely to communicate what we dislike about our partner than what we like.

4. **Jealousy.** The modern disease. It can range from looking too long at a pretty face in the street to adultery.

5. **Money.** Different spending priorities are always difficult, but the new twist is discovery your partner has accumulated large credit card debts.

6. **Chores.** Not only who does what, but how long it takes to get around to it. Whose turn it is to empty the dishwasher and how it was stacked in the first place are popular sparring topics.

7. **Sex.** One partner has "gone off" sex—leaving the other bewildered and angry.

8. **Children.** Different ideas about discipline and what is appropriate at which age. For example: preteens wanting to dress provocatively.

9. **Space.** Traditionally it's been men who've wanted time to themselves, but women burdened by work and kids are asking for "me" time too.

10. **In-laws.** Nobody likes unasked-for advice, especially when it comes from his or her parents.

## WHY ARGUING IS GOOD FOR YOUR RELATIONSHIP

Couples like to think that they have integrity and generally tell each other the truth. One partner might pretend, for example, that the new home movie theater cost a little less, or the other forgets to mention the stripper at their best friend's hen party, but there are few serious transgressions. Yet when it comes to our feelings, the rules change. We constantly tell white lies to preserve the peace or avoid upsetting our partner. How often have you said: "No problem," "Of course, I don't mind," "It's nothing" when actually you meant the complete opposite? Often a couple will boast "We can tell each other anything," but in reality tell each other close to nothing. Although the truth, both saying it and hearing it, can be scary, emotional honesty will set your relationship free and save it from becoming duller and duller.

We are less likely to consider sex dirty, bad, or something embarrassing to be hidden away. Instead, we have a different forbidden feeling: anger. Except, like sex, anger is a part of being a human and cannot be wished away. Whether we like to admit it or not, everybody gets angry at some time. Unfortunately, many couples are uncomfortable or frightened by anger and therefore develop strategies for keeping conflict at bay. However, all the avoidance strategies not only fail to deal with the underlying anger but ultimately cause more pain than dealing with the anger head-on.

Four common avoidance strategies are detachment, skipping, rationalizing, and blocking.

## Detachment

Couples tell themselves: "It doesn't matter," "We'll agree to differ," and "Ultimately, who cares?" While putting anger in cold storage can work in the short term, this strategy risks freezing over every feeling—even the positive ones. The effect is devastating. Jennifer is a forty-year-old maritime lawyer: "There were things I didn't agree with, important things, but I didn't want to rock the boat. So I didn't say anything, I just shut down, and gradually all my emotions became dulled." Jennifer woke up one day in a passionless marriage and drifting toward divorce without knowing what was wrong.

"The whole focus of our counseling was on teaching us how to argue productively," Jennifer explains. "Although nothing was solved when we were shouting at each other, later when we'd calmed down and had a civilized conversation, we always found a compromise." The roundtable discussions were productive because they had been through a cathartic conflict first. However, this is tough and many couples find themselves trapped in a vicious circle. By not arguing and processing anger, partners will become withdrawn and less likely to communicate—until the only strategy left is to detach.

## EXERCISE    LEARN TO NAME YOUR FEELINGS

Many clients claim not to have many feelings, but the reality is that they are not always aware of their full range. At first, some clients look blank when I ask them to write down as many "feelings" as possible. But I bring in a flip chart and before long we have filled a complete sheet.

1. **How many feelings can you list?** Write as many on a piece of paper and then try and think of some more.

2. **Look at the range of your feelings.** Feelings belong in "families," so circle and connect ones that you think belong together. In my opinion there are probably six main groups:

- **Shock** (which includes surprise, confusion, amazement)

- **Anger** (which includes rage, resentment, frustration, annoyance, irritation, impatience)

- **Sadness** (including grief, disappointment, hurt, and despair)

- **Fear** (including anxiety, worry, insecurity, panic, jealousy, guilt, shame)

- **Love** (which includes acceptance, admiration, appreciation, gratitude, relief, empathy, compassion)

- **Disgust** (including contempt, disdain, aversion, scorn, and revulsion)

- **Happiness** (including joy, fulfillment, satisfaction, pleasure, contentment, and amusement) However, you might find more families or decide some emotions belong in different places. There are no right or wrong choices. Maybe even invest in a thesaurus, because the richer the range of emotions the richer the life.

3. **Understand the complexity of your feelings.** So many of these feelings seem negative—four whole families in fact—and the "love" and "happiness" family are often overlooked during our original brainstorm. However, on closer inspection some of them are neutral, especially in the shock family. The negative ones can have positive sides; for example, there is always passion along with jealousy. Meanwhile, the positive ones have a down side; admiration, for example, can become unquestioning hero worship.

## Skipping

Some couples accept that they will get angry, but because they also feel guilty or uncomfortable push it away as quickly as possible. Anger is normally a wake-up call that something is wrong, but instead of listening to the message hidden beneath the pain these couples skip straight to solving the dispute. Angelina would get home later than her partner, Frank, and immediately start preparing the evening meal. If she were late, she would ask him to help chop up vegetables or cube meat. Although Frank was willing to help, it nearly always ended up with one or other of them getting angry. Sometimes she would skip the row by trying to second-guess what his problem might be. "No wonder, you're so slow—that knife needs sharpening," she would tell him; or "You're fed up because your favorite cutting board is still in the dishwasher." Alternatively, he would try to solve the problem on the spot: "You've had a hard time at work, go and put your feet up." As soon as anger appeared on the scene, Frank and Angelina tried to avoid the argument by heading for the exit sign. These suggestions might have been made with love, but by skipping over the anger they had found only superficial answers.

In counseling, we unpacked the layers beneath cutting boards and tiredness. Angelina felt that a good wife should have prepared a hot meal by a certain time; Frank was able to reassure her that he was more flexible. However, there was more to their rows that this—the couple had very rigid ideas of what men and women did in a relationship. Nevertheless, Angelina felt that she was doing the lion's share of the household chores and wanted more help. Meanwhile, Frank feared that she wanted to order him around—rather like the site supervisor at his job. Although he was willing to do more at home, he did not want the same dynamics as at work. By no longer skipping the anger, Angelina and Frank discovered the layers of the argument and a proper solution.

## **EXERCISE** KEEP A FEELINGS DIARY

For a week, whenever you have a spare few minutes, jot down any feeling that you have experienced. In could be on the train, when your next appointment is running late, or watching your kids playing. Write all your feelings, even the ones that feel uncomfortable—in fact especially those. This is a private diary, so be emotionally honest with yourself. You don't have to do anything with these feelings, just be aware of them and practice naming them.

When unsure of our emotions, we try to keep them down at the mild end of the spectrum for fear of being overwhelmed. Yet most people feel something a notch or two up from what they first report. So next time you write down, for example, that you are upset, try to be more honest and move further up the scale to the hidden emotions like anxiety, disappointment, or resentment.

Looking back over your diary entries, ask yourself, am I experiencing every group of feelings: shock, anger, sadness, fear, love, disgust, happiness? If one family is particularly underrepresented it is important to understand why. Did your parents have trouble experiencing these feelings? Why should you be inhibited? Next, deliberately look out for these emotions—even if they all come from the mild end. For example, if you feel very little from the love/joy family, make certain you record the small pleasures. If you see a beautiful flower or smile at a cartoon in your social media feed write down "happy" or "content."

## Rationalizing

While feelings are generally located in the body—for example, love seems an ache in the chest and fear a sinking sensation in the stomach—rationalizing keeps everything logical, plausible, and in the head.

Nick and Anna sought counseling after he fell out of love with her. They preferred to describe their arguments as "heated discussions" and tried to neutralize any dispute by questioning each other's logic rather than addressing any underlying anger. A typical example would be the time Nick elbowed Anna in bed during the night. "He attacked me," she complained. "I hardly think 'attacked,'" countered Nick, "That suggests an element of premeditation." Anna was straight back with: "I'm not allowed to have an opinion now?" Their feelings were not being addressed as the argument quickly became about language, all conducted in the most reasonable and rational voices. By Nick and Anna's standards it was a nasty fight, but they were both still unsatisfied and quietly seething.

So we started to unpack the real issues. The elbow in the back, during a restless night, symbolized what Anna saw as Nick's uncaring attitude. But because she wanted him to stay, she was determined to be "sweetness and light." The feeling still had to come out somehow, and this "heated discussion" was a subconscious attempt by Anna to deal with some of the frustration. If they had both lost their tempers, Anna would probably have blurted out the truth about holding back her feelings. By keeping everything very rational, they were protecting themselves from not only raised voices, but also a proper understanding of their relationship's dynamics and a lasting solution.

# **EXERCISE** DISTINGUISH BETWEEN FEELINGS AND THOUGHTS

Just putting "I feel" at the beginning of a sentence does not make someone emotionally honest. For example: "I feel you were wrong" or "I feel you were out of order." Both sentences tell us nothing about the emotions of the person talking. We could guess disappointment, perhaps, but maybe frustration or even contempt. What the speaker has expressed is an opinion.

1. **Feelings often come from our body.** We have a physical reaction: a tightening of the chest; a sinking in the stomach; the heart beating faster; trembling.

2. **Thoughts come from our head.** They are opinions, ideas, judgments, and beliefs. This does not make them any less valid but they are not feelings.

3. **Report the feelings.** Once you have become fluent identifying and naming feelings in your diary move onto telling your partner. Sometimes just acknowledging the feeling to yourself will make you less on edge. In some cases, you will no longer even feel the need to tell your partner, but if you do decide to tackle them, make certain to follow the next point.

4. **Own the feeling.** "I feel" rather than "you make me feel." For example, "I feel angry (infuriated, frustrated, or whatever) when you don't put the cap back on properly on the orange juice." Rather than "You make me angry with your thoughtlessness." The more specific the complaint, the less it seems like an attack on someone's personality. After all, it is much easier to change our behavior—putting out the plastic bottles—than our personality.

## Blocking

One half gets angry, but the other half simply refuses to engage with their anger. The blocking partner will walk away, bury himself or herself in work and household chores, or just hide behind watching TV or checking social media. Generally, Sian and Steven could solve their differences, but there was one topic that completely overwhelmed their coping skills. Steven had two large dogs, which had been specially bred to retrieve objects from water, and at the weekend he would be off at competitions. Sian was not a dog person and certainly not a large, wet, hairy dog person, so the dogs lived in a kennel outside. However, the potential for disagreements about Steven's hobby were endless. If Sian ever tried to tackle him about them, Steven would either be silent and just let her rant or walk out of the room. Sian would be left fuming—brimming over with anger. Although Steven would get angry, and perhaps slam a door, none of it would be expressed directly to Sian.

## EXERCISE   LISTENING ATTENTIVELY

In the same way that you expect your partner to be attentive to your feelings, be prepared to offer the same respect back.

1. Do not interrupt OR try to minimize your partner's feelings, and don't tell him or her not to feel that way.

2. Acknowledge what has been said, even if it has been hard to hear. A responsible way to handle this, without taking all the blame would be: "I feel sad that you say that I ..." Another good way to acknowledge is to summarize what you have just heard: "So what you're saying is ..."

3. Remember: a greater awareness of feelings leads to a richer life, with not only a better understanding of yourself, but better empathy with your partner and improved people skills all around.

## Unprocessed Anger

Some people are so determined to mask their anger—because "good people don't get mad"—that it has nowhere to go but inward. Ultimately, the anger turns into headaches, ulcers, nervous conditions, depression, or self-harm. The other costs of masked anger are not getting what you want and low self-respect.

If anger is not expressed, or swallowed, it will begin to seep out. Instead of direct criticism—which could either be challenged or maybe taken on board and acted on—there are snide comments and put-downs. Jilly, a forty-five-year-old marketing assistant, found low-grade resentment was ruining her life: "He'd make sarcastic comments like 'wonderful' and 'of course Princess,' when I wanted, for example, to go out with my girlfriends. But if I challenged him, he'd just say something like: 'Can't I even have an opinion now?' It was impossible to pin him down. Did he object to my night on the town, what I was wearing, or was he just jealous? Who knows? We'd just end up bickering all the time." Behind each sarcastic comment are several unspoken opinions and again so many different layers. Is it any wonder neither party knows what they are really discussing or where they truly stand?

Instead of directly confronting issues some people either consciously or unconsciously play games. It is sneaky anger because, on the surface, they seem cooperative but they never get round to what they were asked. They "forget" to make phone calls, put off home improvement projects to next weekend, or deliberately load the dishwasher incorrectly—so their partner does not ask again. Psychologists call this sort of behavior passive-aggressive. While anger explodes and can potentially clear the air, passive aggression hangs around poisoning a relationship. As children, these people were often told not to yell, talk back, lose their temper, argue, or rebel. In effect their parents were saying "Let's pretend these feelings and impulses don't exist in me and I'll pretend they don't exist in you."

Passive-aggressive adults always have a million excuses which make the real issues harder and harder to tackle. Mark, a thirty-seven-year-old local government officer, would agree to do something for his partner but actually felt anything but cooperative: "I'd smile to her face and agree 'of course it was my turn to empty the laundry basket,' but I'd never quite get round to doing it." Eventually his partner retaliated and stopped doing things for him too. Having reached stalemate, they started counseling where Mark learned to be honest about his feelings, rather than sneakily hiding his anger away. Finally they could properly negotiate who did what, rather than snipe at each other. Other games played by the passive-aggressive include: "Oops I forgot," "Yes but ..." (add your own excuse), acting dumb and helpless, and sulking. In the meantime, their partner's patience snaps and she or he loses their temper. The passive-aggressive person will then turn self-righteous and blame their partner for the upset.

## EXERCISE   HOW TO DEAL WITH A PASSIVE AGGRESSOR

1. Ask yourself, why can't my partner assert himself or herself directly? Passive aggression is normally the choice of people who feel powerless. Is your partner allowed to say no?

2. Bring the hidden hostility up to the surface. Challenge any too easy agreement: "I don't think you want to ..." Don't feel guilty or allow yourself to be manipulated into apologizing for having got angry or annoyed.

3. Avoid misunderstandings. Repeat back instructions, set precise deadlines, and at work establishing penalties for procrastination.

4. Once you've made a stand, follow through. If someone is always late and you've told them you'll leave if they are more than ten minutes late and haven't called, then make certain you do. Failure to carry out the penalties will severely weaken your position.

## **EXERCISE** HOW TO STOP BEING PASSIVELY AGGRESSIVE

**1.** Accept that anger is normal.

**2.** Accept that you can still be a good person even when you feel angry.

**3.** Look at the benefits of using anger well. It gets things done and rights wrongs.

**4.** Understand your fears about being angry. What is the worst that could happen? What strategies could you use that will allow you to be angry but circumnavigate these fears?

**5.** Old behaviors, even if they worked for you as a child, will need updating. Unlike a kid, who has to go to school whether they like it or not, you have choices.

**6.** Practice saying no. It cuts through a lot of passive-aggressive behavior. If there is a row at least both of you know what you are fighting about, instead of your anger being masked by sneaky behavior.

**7.** Tell your partner when you feel pushed around.

# BREAKING FREE FROM
# A LOW-CONFLICT RELATIONSHIP

Having looked at the pain and problems caused by denying arguments, it is time to turn to look at constructive arguments. When I explain this concept to my clients one partner will often say: "This is all very well but I don't want to just pick a fight." The other will chip in: "It all seems so artificial." So let's be clear. I am not suggesting becoming needlessly confrontational or arguments for the sake of arguments. Every day we are given invitations to get angry: someone cuts in front of the car; our call is not returned; we are given unfair criticism. What I ask is that next time an argument is brewing not to sidestep it.

Some clients, who are very uncomfortable with conflict, start gently either with strangers or work colleagues. Angelina, who avoided arguments over preparing the evening meal, could feel herself getting angry with a store assistant who was too busy talking to a colleague to serve her. "Normally I would stand there and fume inside," she explained, "but this time I could feel my teeth clenching and I thought go for it. I was surprised how calm I sounded when I said: 'Excuse me, could you help me.'" The second surprise for Angelina was that there was no smart comment or come back from the assistant. "It turned out to be no big deal," she told me. After practicing on strangers, she was ready to be honest with Frank too. Angelina might have recognized her invitation to get angry, but many couples have become so adept at avoiding issues that they forget the signs.

## **EXERCISE** THE SEVEN SIGNS THAT YOU NEED AN ARGUMENT

Look at the list below and ask yourself: How many invitations to be angry have I ignored?

**1.** One partner is more silent than usual.

**2.** Body language: not looking each other in the eye; hunched shoulders; crossed arms; tense jaw; tapping your foot or pacing around.

**3.** Voice pitch changes: tension in the vocal chords makes them tighter and the sounds more brittle.

**4.** Taking offense easily: "Why did you do that?"

**5.** Repeatedly checking with each other: "Are you OK?" "Everything all right?"—but receiving a sharp or irritated response.

**6.** Pointless contradicting: "No, I don't agree," "Are you sure?"

**7.** Things that you have put up with for ages, without complaint, suddenly start grating.

## SUMMING UP

Arguments are necessary for solving the inevitable conflicts between two people in a loving relationship. However, many couples are frightened of having rows in case they spin out of control. Destructive strategies for keeping anger at bay include detaching, skipping, rationalizing, and blocking. Unfortunately, trying to avoid anger can cause more problems.

## IN A NUTSHELL:

- Be open and honest about your feelings. It is the foundation for good communication.

- Ducking an invitation to argue might be easier in the short term but it stores up problems for the future.

- Although rows are never nice, they do provide an opportunity to solve long-standing issues.

# CHAPTER FIVE

---

# High-Conflict Relationships

Anger is a double-edged sword. On one side, it is a gift—providing the energy to get things done, redress injustice, and sort out problems. On the other, anger can get us into a lot of trouble. Understanding the differences and harnessing the positive elements of anger is one of the most important relationship skills; unfortunately, it is also one of the most difficult.

There are two types of high-conflict relationship couples who seek my help. For the first group, anger has always been a problem—either the couple fight like cat and dog or one partner is almost permanently angry and the other tiptoeing around the next row. For the second group, there is a particular unsolved problem that has turned nasty and consumed all the goodwill until it is impossible to talk about anything without the conversation degenerating into threats, name-calling, and one partner getting upset, making the other upset, and setting off a spiral of bitterness and despair. Even the happiest relationships sometimes have arguments where anger gets out of hand and one, but normally both, partners get hurt. So what is the answer?

The best place to start is understanding the differences between the positive and negative sides of anger. Healthy anger is when we recognize a real problem, act on it, and then let it go once the issue is resolved. Most importantly, the anger is also in proportion to the offense. In sharp contrast, anger becomes a problem when someone represses it (because they can't deal with it) and then explodes with rage (getting angrier than is appropriate or necessary) or likes anger too much (because it makes them feel powerful and helps them get their own way). While there is only one type of healthy anger—more about this at the end of the chapter—there are six types of negative anger. After each one below, there is an exercise specifically designed to help breakout of this anger style.

## SUDDEN ANGER

This kind of anger arrives quickly and dissipates quickly. Although these people get rid of their frustrations, they end up saying terrible things. Once they have cooled down, and registered the reactions and impact on their nearest and dearest, they feel ashamed, guilty, and determined not to let it happen again—until the next time. So what's going on?

Because people prone to sudden anger do not like anger in themselves or others, they ignore the triggers that make everybody else annoyed. However, instead of dealing with the issues, they grit their teeth, deny their feelings, and carry on. Unfortunately, the feelings do not disappear and the frustration and the pressure build up to such an intolerable level that they explode.

For example, Virginia would, as her partner Gordon described it, go ballistic. She would yell, swear, and even throw things—such as the breakfast bowl he'd put in the sink rather than the dishwasher. Inside his head, Gordon would dismiss his partner as "a moody cow." But because Virginia had denied all the previous irritations, Gordon was not aware of the thousand other things that had broken down her composure—just the final straw. From his viewpoint, her anger had no rhyme or reason: "I'd forgotten to put my bowl away hundreds of times before and she'd not reacted like that—totally out of all proportion to the crime." Most people with sudden anger issues have high—almost unrealistic—standards for themselves (taking on so much that they are easily stressed) and for other people.

## How to Recognize It

Everybody loses their temper from time to time, but you have a problem when:

🌺 You get angry over "stupid" or petty things that you would generally take in your stride. Worse still, your anger seems to come out of nowhere and it is only in retrospect that you can identify the pressure points.

🌺 Instead of feeling better that issues are out in the open, you feel worse, guilty, or stupid and your partner and family are upset.

🌺 Your body language can turn very aggressive. You tap your feet, start pacing, keep sighing, try to work faster (to distract yourself), and start slamming things down.

🌺 When someone asks "What's the matter?" this will raise rather than lower the tension.

🌺 Instead of solving problems, your anger has become one of the stumbling blocks.

## EXERCISE  SLOWING DOWN YOUR ANGER

Instead of going from zero to one hundred in a few seconds, slow down your reactions, understand the triggers better, and head off the worst of the crisis.

**Monitor your body:** Become aware of the tension in your head, neck, and shoulders. What's happening in your stomach or across your chest? Have your eyes narrowed? What about your hands or feet? Has your voice changed? How?

**Keep an anger diary:** Write down everything that is making you angry or has made you angry in the run-up to a sudden explosion. What are the patterns? How do you describe yourself in your private thoughts: A victim? A saint? Have you jumped to conclusions? Do you feel people deserve your anger?

**Deal with the stress:** Breathe slowly and deeply. Relax your face and body, and stop pacing. Tell yourself you will communicate better if you're calmer. Check that you are using your normal voice. Let the anger drain away.

**Take responsibility:** It is your job to avoid an explosion—not other people's to calm you down. How can you soothe yourself? What makes you feel better? Going for a walk? A round of golf? Having a bath? Cleaning?

**Resolve the issue:** When you have cooled down, look at the triggers and find the fundamental problems that are driving your anger. Once out of the red zone, it is tempting to sidestep or downgrade problems, but this just provides fuel for the next outburst. Instead, use the skills in the next chapter to talk to your partner and resolve any outstanding issues.

## HABITUAL ANGER

These people are constantly angry and, most of the time cannot put their finger on exactly why. Many people with habitual anger will have always been grumpy, irritated quickly, and generally, been on a short fuse. They learned as children that tantrums got their parent's attention; they might not necessarily have got what they wanted but even negative attention was better than none at all. More commonly, habitual anger is a sign that a relationship has been in trouble for a long time. Nothing seems to resolve any of the couple's problems and they settle down into trench warfare where anything can set off another round of fireworks and afterward each partner retreats to the relative safety of their bunkers.

Rebecca was angry all the time with her partner Daniel and vice versa. In order to break the deadlock, I facilitated a discussion about finding one nice thing that each could do for the other. Daniel would have liked a coffee in the morning. "It's not fair, I have to get up early and I haven't go time to run after him," Rebecca replied. There followed a debate about whether she could put the kettle on the stove before she left—so it would be ready when Daniel came down. "But what if the kettle was empty? I'm really pressed for time," she complained. "So you can't even do that," said Daniel. "I knew you'd turn this into another stick to beat me," countered Rebecca.

Daniel had just as many excuses for his nice thing for Rebecca—buying bread for her sandwiches—and it soon became clear this conversation was going nowhere. "What are you both so angry about?" I asked. They paused for a moment, perplexed, and then launched into a list of complaints, but they weren't answering my question. They were too habitually angry to look beneath the surface.

## How to Recognize It

You can tell your anger has turned into a habit when:

- It feels normal to be angry and outbursts happen almost automatically.

- You feel pessimistic most of the time and especially about your partner's ability to change.

- You have high expectations of other people and they generally let you down.

- You are too mad, too quickly, and for too long.

## **EXERCISE**  **THE ANGER PYRAMID**

The best way to stop anger being an automatic habit is understanding what fuels it and how different issues interlock.

**1.** Imagine an upside-down pyramid filled with things that make you angry.

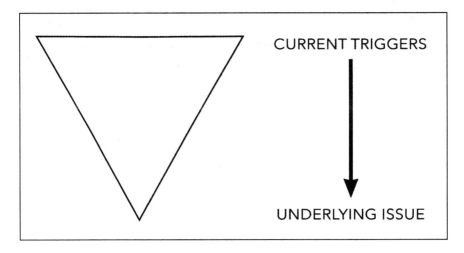

CURRENT TRIGGERS

UNDERLYING ISSUE

Across the top are all the current triggers—for example, Rebecca and Daniel would put *buying bread* or *making coffee*.

**2.** What drives those immediate issues goes in the layer underneath, and so on.

**3.** To get down from the multitude of minor issues at the top, to the overriding issue at the bottom, take one of the immediate triggers and ask:

"Why does [for example] making coffee in the morning make me angry?"

Rebecca answered: *Because I have to get up so early.*

**4.** Take your answer and repeat the question:

"Why does ... getting up early ... make me angry?"

Rebecca answered: *Because he's still lying in bed.*

**5.** Keep repeating the process:

"Why does ... Daniel lying in bed ... make me angry?"
Rebecca answered: *I have to work so hard.*

"Why does ... working so hard ... make me angry?"
Rebecca answered: *I have to earn the lion's share of the money.*

"Why does ... earning the lion's share ... make me angry?"

**6.** Stop when you find something new or surprising.

Rebecca answered: *I want to give up work and have a baby.*

**7.** Turn this discovery from a statement into a question:

*How can we afford to have a baby?*

Rebecca and Daniel finally had the underlying issue driving their habitual anger and instead of scrapping over trivia could really begin to talk.

---

## SHAME-BASED ANGER

These people have a low opinion of themselves. Their parents, teachers, and society in general have given them the message that they are not "good enough." Fortunately, they have found a way of coping day-to-day with this pain. Unfortunately, it is making the situation worse. So what is happening?

Firstly, they deny how they feel deep down and cover up by being either arrogant ("I'm better than everybody else") or perfectionists ("I can only feel good about myself if I'm perfect"). Unfortunately, people suffering from shame-based anger can never quite persuade themselves that they really are better than anybody else, so even the slightest criticism brings their whole act tumbling down. These are the people who, if you correct a spelling mistake, will explode and flounce off: "If you don't want my help ...." They have such a poor opinion of themselves that anything less than a standing ovation seems like a rebuke. It also goes without saying that nobody can be perfect all the time. So there is a lot of fuel for anger being carried about.

Some people turn the destructive feeling inward (like self-harming or self-sabotage), but more commonly, and this is the second problem with this coping strategy, they take it out on other people. As a child, Simon felt his mother preferred his brother and indeed she often said he would "never amount to anything." As an adult, Simon was naturally very sensitive to criticism (and could be perceived as arrogant by his colleagues). In his first counseling session, he listed some of the incentive trips and prizes that he had won as salesman of the month. The couple had financial problems—since Amanda had given up working after the birth of their second child—and if the subject of money came up, Simon would immediately start bristling: "I follow up every lead, I'm even on the phone in the evening trying to earn more commission." Amanda would try to clarify: "I'm just saying we have to decide on our spending priorities." It was too late, Simon was straight into attack mode: "What about the state of the house? It's no pleasure to come home to toys all over the place and diaper-changing stuff in the middle of the living room. It's not hygienic ...." Simon believed it was better to attack than be attacked and on many occasions it worked—Amanda was scared off and left him alone. Unfortunately, it was also ruining his marriage.

## How to Recognize It

This is an easier fault to recognize in other people than ourselves—and I meet many couples where both partners are equally guilty—so look at the following and ask whether you have fallen into this trap too.

- ❧ You judge yourself so harshly, you expect other people to do the same. Can you hear criticism when none was intended? Do you overreact?

🌱 Do you ever wonder if someone knew the "real you" they would stop loving you or abandon you? (By trying to cover up your supposed faults, you are actually becoming unlovable and feeding your fears of being abandoned.)

🌱 Shame and blame have become inextricably linked.

🌱 You keep a mental score sheet and feel powerful in victory and overwhelmed when defeated. For this reason, compromises are hard to find.

🌱 When challenged about your anger, you either think it is justified ("after what he or she did") or that everybody is getting at you ("poor me").

## EXERCISE STOP COUNTER-COMPLAINING

When one partner brings up an issue but the other counters it with another problem, the situation can quickly degenerate into a row about dozens of issues with each one becoming harder to solve. Try this four-step plan:

### 1. Break the connection between shame and blame

- If you haven't started one already, keep an anger diary.

- Write down what people say or do that triggers your shame. Compare what someone actually said against what you heard. Have you added extra interpretations? Is your reaction more about you than them?

- What type of people trigger your shame-based anger? Are they in positions of authority, colleagues, or somebody in a lower position? Sometimes, the people we meet today are standing in for someone from the past or allowing us to relive old patterns. For example, problems with authority figures could be about your parents, or irritating colleagues could be replacing a bothersome brother or sister. When becoming angry with store assistants or subordinates at work, we are replaying how we were treated by our parents or teachers, but compensating by taking the more powerful role.

- Understand how you convert shame to anger. Do you shout? Do you put people down? Do you nit-pick?

## 2. Make a commitment to change

- Double-check if someone really meant to shame you. In most cases, you will have overreacted.

- Develop a new internal voice that counters the dark ones from the past. For example, when your employer stops by your desk remind yourself: my boss is not my father. This will stop their comments being filtered through old scripts.

- When you find yourself about to cross-complain, mentally pause and count to ten.

## 3. Heal your shame

- Build your self-respect on firmer foundations. Rather than basing your self-worth on what other people think, start to value your own opinions and beliefs more. There is more about this in another of my books, *Learn to Love Yourself Enough*.

- However, rest assured, understanding the links between the past and today is half the journey to greater self-esteem.

- Learn to accept criticism as a gift. Someone has offered you a chance to grow or see yourself through their eyes. (Remember, you don't have to take everything on board— there might be some parts that you still feel are unjust, but concentrate on the useful things you could adopt.)

## 4. Treat others with respect

- Instead of looking for things to criticize, start looking for things to praise.

- Stop ignoring your partner when he or she has something to say—by walking away or burying yourself in a computer game or TV show—and start listening.

- The better you treat your partner, the more respect they will have for you.

---

# PARANOID ANGER

These people are excessively suspicious. They are certain other people are trying to hurt or do them down and therefore never let their guard down. In the worst cases, they follow their partner around, cross-examine their movements, and search for proof of fidelity by monitoring texts and emails or listening in on phone calls. Although someone with paranoid anger will be anxious and upset most of the time, they do not generally express it. Unfortunately, this makes them quick to read anger in other people and to interpret their partner's behavior and words in the worst possible light. I call this negative mind-reading.

When Zoe moved into Derek's apartment she found a box of photographs recording all his golden moments with his ex-girlfriend. "In my defense, they were on the book case—so it's not like I went hunting. I had a quick look when he was out and became transfixed by the sheer number. They couldn't have a glass of wine without a snap shot. I wouldn't mind, except he hardly ever takes a photo of us." When she tackled Derek, he said he would put them up in the attic. This did not satisfy Zoe: "If you really loved me, you would have destroyed them. I certainly haven't kept any old photographs of my boyfriends." This is typical of negative mind-reading—there could be lots of innocent reasons why they were in his bookcase. "To be honest, I'd forgotten all about them," explained Derek, "I don't really want to destroy them because they're a record of past vacations." Zoe interpreted this as a sign that he was still in love with her.

Like many people with paranoid anger, in the heat of the row, Zoe would react first and think second. This meant that she often went off hastily and ended up regretting a lot of what she said.

## How to Recognize It

While everyone can jump to the wrong conclusions, it turns into paranoid anger when:

- ❧ Instead of jealousy being a sign that something is wrong with a relationship—like an affair—it goes on forever, whatever the explanation and reassurance from your partner.

- ❧ The feelings are very intense and people become more upset than the situation really merits.

- ❧ In the worst cases, it becomes obsessive and someone can think of very little else.

## EXERCISE HOW TO KICK THE SURVEILLANCE HABIT

**1.** Accept that it is addictive and counterproductive.

**2.** If you are tempted, distract yourself for ten minutes by phoning a friend, reading the paper, or fixing something nice for supper. In most cases, the urge will disappear.

**3.** What are you really trying to achieve? In most cases, a snooper wants reassurance. Instead of getting negative attention through a fight, ask for something positive like a cuddle.

**4.** If you tend to overanalyze every event, try writing down all your thoughts. Don't censor, just get everything down on paper. Next, go through and cross off the exaggerations and strange leaps of logic. What is left? Normally, there are one or two small but manageable fears that need to be talked through with your partner.

5. Discuss what is acceptable access to each other's movements, phone, etc. and what is unreasonable.

# DELIBERATE ANGER

While the previous anger styles are driven by largely unconscious feelings, these people are only too aware of what they are doing and why. They come from angry families and learned from a young age that people who rant and rave often get their own way. Not only can someone with deliberate anger switch it on and off, but will often exaggerate to get their own way.

When I was a student, I lived in an apartment block that opened off a central staircase. One afternoon, while returning home, I heard something being thrown above and shouting. When I reached the third landing, there was a woman picking up some broken crockery while her boyfriend fumed about her stupidity. Embarrassed, I looked the other way as I climbed past. However, the man stopped shouting, greeted me in a normal voice, and tried both to normalize and make me complicit with a "What can you do" shrug. By the time I reached my floor, he was screaming with rage again. He sounded out of control but, in reality, he could switch his anger off and on again.

An example of how deliberate anger is exaggerated comes from Emily, twenty-six. If her husband, Adam, was more than ten minutes late, she would fly into a rage, crying and accusing him of not loving her. "If he truly loved me, he would know how important it is to me and not treat me so badly," she explained. Later in her counseling, Emily admitted that she did not always start off feeling angry. Sometimes she had been busy and not noticed the time. "When I stopped and thought about it, I turned angrier and angrier: 'How dare he. After everything I do for him.'" Although Emily had deliberately switched on her anger, the burst of energy and the accompanying adrenaline rush had tipped her feelings from deliberate into real anger. In the worst cases, deliberate anger can become addictive.

## How to Recognize It

This kind of anger is about power and control and it is very common for both someone using deliberate anger and their partner to minimize the impact on their relationship and hope it will somehow get better. So be truthful when answering these questions. The first section is for someone using deliberate anger:

- Do you find it very hard to be vulnerable and let other people get too close for fear of being hurt?

- Do you use anger to avoid difficult and complicated feelings? By contrast, does anger feel pure and righteous?

- Is "respect" more important to you than to most people?

- Did you witness domestic violence as a child or were you physically abused yourself?

- Are there times when your partner is frightened and fears that you might harm her or him?

- In your heart of hearts, do you know this behavior is not acceptable and is incompatible with a happy relationship?

For the partners of someone using deliberate anger:

- Are you sometimes frightened of your partner and feel controlled?

- Does this somehow seem normal because your partner's behavior corresponds to something you witnessed as a child?

- In a milder form, deliberate anger uses tears and "poor me" behavior to manipulate, but often it will involve abusive language, throwing things, shoving, and slapping. This is domestic violence and is not acceptable.

## **EXERCISE** STOPPING USING DELIBERATE ANGER

At the milder end of this issue—where there is no violence—it is possible to break free on your own, but many people need professional help as well.

1. **Understand the payoffs.** What are the benefits in the short term? What about the medium term? Are they outweighed by the problems in the long term?

2. **Make a commitment to change.** Write it down, as this will make your commitment more real and sign it. Don't make the commitment on the back of a terrible argument, when you are trying to win back your partner, but as a calm, rational response to a pattern of behavior that is not acceptable.

3. **Run your own life and let your partner run her or his life.** This will dramatically reduce the stress and reduce your anger. In the next chapter, there are constructive ways—rather than bullying or nagging—to achieve change.

4. **If you need distance, ask for it.** Many people deliberately pick fights because they need time away. Break this habit by taking up a hobby that allows you time on your own. For example, going fishing, walking a dog, or going to the gym. If you know that a whole weekend together is too much, build in small blocks of time alone.

## MORAL ANGER

One of the main problems with negative anger is that it builds and builds and arguments become more and more destructive. This next style is a sure sign that a couple have tipped from manageable—although still unpleasant—arguments into something nasty and toxic.

Someone with moral anger is always on the "good side" of an argument. Their values are truths. When their partner disagrees, their points are not only dismissed but considered "wrong," "bad," or even "evil" and their opinions are "lies." It goes without saying that someone with moral anger is judgmental and easily disappointed by other people. However, and this is this the most insidious twist, because their partner is so clearly wrong, they clearly "deserve" to be punished, pulled down a peg, or belittled. The other partner fights back and this behavior is used to justify another bout of moral anger.

When Gretchen couldn't stand yet another tirade from her husband, she walked out of the house. "She left behind two small children," complained Graham, "she is a clearly not a good mother." With this black and white thinking, he dismissed Gretchen's views. "I left them with their father and I only walked around the block to clear my head," she explained. However, Graham used this incident to reduce the money he transferred each month to the household account. "As she can't be trusted to put the interests of the children first, she can't be trusted with money."

## How to Recognize It

Anger and moral certainty is a very dangerous combination. How many of the following statements, about your partner, do you agree with?

♥ I'm better than you.

♥ I know what's right better than you.

♥ I have better values than you.

♥ I'm right and you're wrong.

Even if you agreed with only one statement, this can be cause for alarm. However, the next two chapters will provide strategies for changing your thinking, learning to listen, and improving communication with your partner. Meanwhile, the following exercise will help you, whatever your anger style, to find a sense of proportion.

# EXERCISE　ANGER THERMOMETER

One of the problems with high-conflict relationships is that couples often overreact and become angrier than the offense demands. Therefore it helps to know, and name, all the graduations from calm up to apoplectic.

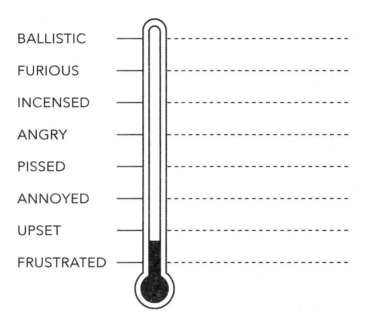

BALLISTIC

FURIOUS

INCENSED

ANGRY

PISSED

ANNOYED

UPSET

FRUSTRATED

Everybody has a different anger thermometer, so I have put a general one down the left-hand side and the right-hand side is blank for you. How would you describe your graduations? If you find anger difficult to express, you might like to add extra items at that end of the scale. If you are too quick to express your anger, you might need more at the other end.

Next time you argue, think where your feelings are on the thermometer. Ask yourself: Have I over- or underestimated my rating? If so, where do I really belong? Let your partner know your thermometer reading as she or he might have misread the signs.

To help you find the right degrees of anger, here is a list of possibilities. Please feel free to add your own ideas.

| | | | |
|---|---|---|---|
| ticked off | bothered | unhappy | impatient |
| offended | bitter | snappy | vengeful |
| disturbed | sulky | indignant | picky |
| hateful | irritated | snarling | troubled |
| miffed | resentful | displeased | glowering |
| riled | spiteful | sore | stewing |

## HEALTHY ANGER

With so many different styles of negative anger, it is important to remember the positive benefits of anger. Here are the six tests as to whether your anger is positive:

1. It is treated as a signal that there is a problem that needs to be addressed.

2. The anger is expressed is proportionate (to the offense) and timely (when the issue occurs, rather than weeks later).

3. The goal is to solve problems rather than just express the anger or let off steam.

4. You own and take responsibility for the anger. "I am angry because …" rather than "You are making me angry."

5. You express the anger in clear ways, so that your partner can respond accordingly.

6. You let go of the anger once the problem is solved.

## What to Do About an Angry Partner

The main thrust of this chapter has been about helping people with their negative anger styles, but what if you are on the receiving end? It is easy to criticize our partner and overlook our own contribution. Remembering that most issues are "six of one and half a dozen of the other" (see Chapter One), could you be unwittingly encouraging your partner to become angrier and turn healthy anger into one of the negative anger styles? Once your partner has cooled down, do you listen, discuss and address the issues, or keep quiet for fear of more arguments? Nothing is solved by avoiding conflict, and more anger is stored away for next time round.

When there is another angry outburst, don't lose your temper too—but try to react with calmness, hear him or her out, and respond with moderation (challenge any "all or nothing" thinking). If your partner gets so angry that these tactics fail, it is probably because she or he has reached fever pitch. In the same way that there is no point reasoning with a drunk, it is counterproductive to argue with someone who has gone ballistic. When your partner is rational again, explain how his or her anger impacts on you. If he or she brushes off your concerns or rationalizes the problem away, stick to your point and explain in further detail the effect on the family and how anger is making it harder to resolve your differences.

Finally, adopt a positive attitude to anger yourself and learn the positive ways to communicate in the next chapter. Little changes in your behavior can have a big knock-on effect on your relationship.

# SUMMING UP

Although anger can be positive, it makes us uncomfortable and many people suppress their feelings. Unfortunately, the anger is still there and bursts out in one or more of the six negative forms. However, by slowing down our automatic reactions, understanding what triggers rows, and learning to express emotions in an appropriate manner, negative anger can be transformed into healthy anger.

## IN A NUTSHELL:

- Accept anger as normal part of life and of being human.

- If your rows become about how you argue and what was said, rather than solving the original trigger, this is a sign of negative anger styles.

- Improving how you handle anger will provide a positive role model for your partner and dramatically improve your communication.

# CHAPTER SIX

---

# Develop Your Assertiveness

So far, you have taken stock of your relationship (and began to identify some of the underlying problems). Next, I explained how avoiding arguments stores up problems for the future and how to deal with anger. In this chapter, we come to the perhaps the most important love hack: assertiveness.

Unfortunately, we are not born with the necessary skills for open and honest communication. It takes until we are about five or six to develop the ability to think through a problem, consider the opinions and feelings of others, and learn enough language to negotiate. Up to this point, a small child has two options. The first is to be a people-pleaser and go along with what Mommy or Daddy wants—which guarantees our parents' love but does not necessarily mean that we get what we want. The second is to become aggressive and demanding (this can involve temper tantrums, tears, wheedling, sulking, and grabbing). It is very effective for getting what we want, but puts up a barrier between us and everybody else.

The children who adopt the people-pleasing option can grow up to be adults who will do anything for a quiet life (and fall into the low-conflict trap). The children who adopt the aggressive or demanding style tend to grow into adults who want to win at any price (and fall into high-conflict trap). Fortunately, there is an alternative: becoming assertive.

Assertiveness training has got a bad name—because many people confuse it with being aggressive. In reality, it goes to the heart of open and honest communication. It is about stating our needs and goals clearly (rather than hiding them behind hints, jokes, or people-pleasing) but being equally aware and respectful of other people's needs and goals (rather than steamrollering over them). Most assertiveness training will start with a list of basic rights but they boil to just three key ones. The good courses will also cover how these rights are balanced by those of our partners.

| MY RIGHTS | MY PARTNER'S RIGHTS |
| --- | --- |
| To ask for what I want | To refuse your request |
| To be listened to and taken seriously | To be listened to and taken seriously |
| To be myself and have space/time to develop as an individual | To rely on you for love, support, and consideration |

If you have done an assertiveness course, perhaps for work, you will find that I use similar language but there are some crucial differences. If you haven't, it doesn't matter because I'm going to explain everything.

## WHAT IS ASSERTIVENESS?

There are three ways of approaching conflict, which are underpinned by three different philosophies. I have exaggerated—but only slightly—each position to make it clearer.

🌹 **1. My needs, wants, and beliefs are of lesser importance and yours are of great importance.**

It's not that these people are a complete pushover but they believe that if they make their partner happy, he or she will make them happy too. Of course, they have an opinion on—for example, where to go on vacation—but if they can avoid an argument by going along with their partner it will feed their greater goals: the quiet life, being liked, avoiding other people's anger. I call this approach: passive.

### ☙ 2. My needs, wants, and beliefs are of great importance and your are of lesser importance.

It's not that these people are greedy, selfish, push to the front of the line people—although this can be the case. They often have a perfectly valid reason—or so they think—for having their own way. For example, they are right—children should go to bed at seven o'clock (and all sensible people will agree, look I've done all this research on the Internet and this is what the experts say). Alternatively, their partner seldom expresses an opinion (because they are passive and want to please), so they think: "If he or she doesn't care, we'll do it my way." In assertiveness courses, this way of communicating is called aggressive; but I don't like the term. People can get their own way by being charming. They can also play the martyr—"don't worry about me I'll just sit here alone in the dark"—where they pretend their needs are not important but manipulate others to reach their goals. Passive-aggressive behavior, where someone agrees to their partner's face to do something, but quietly subvert when their back is turned, also fits into this category. I call this style: domineering.

### ☙ 3. My needs, wants, and beliefs are important and so are yours.

You will immediately recognize this option as assertive. Although most couples who I counsel will intellectually sign up for this option, they discover that they have been using a combination of the other two styles. The most common way is domain-specific domination, for example I will be in control of the money and you will control family time. There is a reasonably equitable power balance and these couples rub along fine until there is a crisis (like the death of a parent) or they move onto another phase of life (for example, the children leaving home). I also see couples where one partner has been domineering and the other passive, which has worked equally well for years—seemingly happily. However, the passive partner has been building up a lot of resentment and has inwardly snapped. They end up justifying some domineering behavior—such as an affair—by telling themselves: "After everything I've done for everybody else, I deserve something just for me."

## LOOKING THROUGH ASSERTIVE EYES

Before working on your own behavior, it is always easier to spot overly domineering or passive behavior in other people.

- **Start by looking at work colleagues and friends.** How do they react if someone makes an impossible demand? Do they agree and get stressed from all the extra work? (Passive.) Maybe they fly off the handle? (Domineering.) Perhaps they are accommodating to the person making the demand but take out their frustration on other colleagues? (Combination of passive and domineering.) Hopefully, your colleague will explain their other commitments and negotiate another solution for getting the work done. (Assertive.)

- **Turning to home life, how does your partner or your children react to a request?** What triggers an aggressive or people-pleasing response? In contrast, what triggers an assertive one? Look closely at the differences that generate the positive outcome. What sort of language is used? What about body language and tone of voice?

- **Finally, start observing yourself.** How do you respond to authority figures—such as your doctor, your children's teachers, or the woman taking your yoga class—who say something with which you disagree? Is your natural response to nod and accept it—but inwardly fume? (Passive.) When a sales assistant is rude or annoyed that your perfectly reasonable request is causing extra work, do you become angry and aggressive? (Domineering.) In contrast, how do you feel when you speak your mind but keep your temper under control—so that your reaction is in proportion to the offense? (Assertive.)

# HOW YOUR BODY LANGUAGE GIVES YOU AWAY

When couples in counseling report back on an argument during the week, they are often surprised at how some relatively innocent remark sparked a huge row. However, the problem is not so much what was said, but the manner in which it was expressed. This is because our true feelings leak out through our body language:

## Domineering Body Language

This is shown in the following ways:

- **Posture:** Hands on the hips with elbows pointing out. Aggressive people pull themselves up to their full height to look as tall and dominant as possible.

- **Facial muscles:** A tight, taught look around the face. Gritted teeth. Eyes narrowed. Any smile does not reach the eyes.

- **Movements:** Tense and jerky. Impatience is shown by rubbing hands or tapping feet. Domineering people will stand too close.

- **Gestures:** Finger wagging or clenched fists. Patronizing touching or patting on the shoulder. Short quick nods to say "get on with it."

- **Eye contact:** Staring. No blinking.

- **Tone:** Louder, harsher than usual. By contrast, some people are threateningly quiet.

## Passive Body Language

The following signs should be easy to spot:

- **Posture:** Round shouldered—as if someone is trying to look smaller and less significant. Crossed arms—as if protecting or hugging themselves. When seated, someone with passive body language will almost curl in on themselves.

- **Facial muscles:** A gloomy, overapologetic, pleading look. Chewing lower lip. Chin dropped toward the chest.

- **Movements:** Tense, agitated, fidgeting. People-pleasers will often become clumsy and start dropping things. They will also back away and leave too much distance between themselves and the person speaking.

- **Gestures:** Fiddling with clothes, hair, or pens. The hand covers the mouth and there is lots of face touching. Alternatively, there are few movements or gestures—as if someone is trying to be invisible. This is normally a sign of low self-esteem.

- **Eye contact:** Passive people find it hard to make eye contact. Either, the eyes are lowered or they dart nervously around. Another strategy is to close the eyes for long stretches of time—as if, like an ostrich burying its head in the sand, what they can't see won't hurt them. Alternatively, someone who people-pleases will hang on every word.

- **Tone:** Quiet. The speech is tentative or mumbling. There is also an apologetic or whining note in the voice.

## Assertive Body Language

By contrast, these messages are much more neutral:

- **Posture:** Open. Hands hang loosely by the side or are placed in the lap. Little crossing of arms and legs.

- **Facial muscles:** Relaxed and sincere with plenty of smiles.

- **Movements:** Steady, fluid, and regular. Someone with assertive body language will lean forward to the person speaking—to show interest. Their head is erect in a responsive rather than threatening way.

- **Gestures:** These will match what is being said. There are no intrusive or excessive mannerisms.

🐾 **Eye contact:** Good. Small nods show that the person talking is being heard and encouraged to say more.

🐾 **Tone:** Evenly pitched, steady, and easily heard.

## EXERCISE IMPROVE YOUR BODY LANGUAGE

Draining excess aggression or submission out of your body will not only improve your partner's reactions and reduce miscommunication, but changing your outward posture will also change how you feel inside.

1. **Dealing with anger.** Starting with your toes and feet and moving up your buttocks, fists, shoulders, and face—clench everything. Hold for a second or two. Then, slowly, release all the tension from your muscles. Shake it out and go as limp as the surroundings allow. Finally, take one or two deep breaths.

2. **Go to a beautiful place.** We all have favorite spots. It could be your garden, a stunning view, or a calmness that comes from sustained exercise such as swimming or jogging. Where is your beautiful place? Close your eyes and really make the picture come to life. What details are particularly pleasing? What about the smells? What can you hear? Next time you feel overwhelmed or frightened by the world, superimpose this positive picture over the negative one.

3. **Become more positive.** Adopt an assertive body language. Imagine an upside-down triangle across your partner's eyebrows and nose and keep your eyes fixed on this zone. Sit or lean forward, so you can monitor your partner's response and gauge the effect of your message. Don't hide behind your phone or ask for something you'd like from another room. If you are relaxed and open, your partner will subconsciously match your assertive manner.

## ASSERTIVENESS IN ACTION

There are two elements to assertive communication: good body language, which we have already covered, and building agreement. The following case history illuminates this second point.

Philip and Sophie were both in their early forties and had first met at school. Over the years, Philip's confidence grew as his business took off and made more and more money. This had allowed Sophie to give up her job and concentrate on bringing up their two children. Although she had no regrets about this decision, her confidence and self-esteem went in the opposite direction to Philip's. The couple arrived for their weekly counseling session with thunderous faces. Sophie had spent a lot of time arranging a family barbecue and party: "I'd bought some lights to hang around the pool and spent hours making the garden look special. It had been a long time since we'd had both our families over and I was looking forward to a great weekend. Two days before the party, Philip dropped a bombshell: he'd invited two business colleagues along."

Although, Sophie was furious on the inside, she basically kept quiet: "I didn't want a scene or to spoil the party." This is typical passive behavior. In contrast, Philip was domineering. (The two styles often go hand-in-hand.) "You should have known that they were only in the U.S. for a few days and I would have to entertain them," he said. "Anyway, why on earth did we spend all that money on the garden and pool if it wasn't going to help the business?" This blaming and judgmental language is a hallmark of being domineering. He also upped the stakes with inflammatory remarks: "You don't understand anything" and "If you'd just listen for a change."

Unfortunately, the party had been a disaster; the family did not really have anything to say to the business contacts and tended to talk to each other. Philip thought: "Your family were rude and made guests in my house feel ostracized." Worse still, some of the boys had started dive-bombing the pool and had soaked one of the businessmen.

Instead of standing up for herself and perhaps saying that it had been a mistake to mix two very different sets of people—which would have been assertive—Sophie had used people-pleasing techniques and tried to diffuse Philip's anger with excessive explanation and excuses: "I was having trouble because the hollandaise sauce was curdling. I probably let the bowl get too warm. My sister was telling me a long story about her move, so I couldn't be watching the boys." She was also offering lots of justification: "It's been ages since the family has got together and there was lots of news to catch up on" and "The boys had been cooped up studying for their exams and they need to let off steam." Her final signature passive behavior was overapologizing: "I've said a hundred times, it won't happen again. I've spoken to my sister and she's disciplined her son." Unfortunately, this just made Philip see red: "Can't you even do this one thing right?" Criticism without offering a solution is typical domineering behavior.

Instead of letting this argument go round and round in circles, getting nastier and nastier, I took them through the six ingredients for an assertive discussion where both sides have the right to ask for what they want, to be listened to and taken seriously, and where it is possible to refuse a request:

**Support each other's position.** Sophie said: "I understand that it would be rude to dump them in a strange town over the weekend." Philip said: "I accept that we don't get much time as a family—all together."

**Offer praise.** Sophie said: "You work really hard and I don't tell you enough how proud that I am of all you've achieved." Philip said: "You had the garden looking really nice."

**Build bridges.** Philip said: "I would have preferred it if everybody had mixed." Sophie said: "If I'd had more notice, I could have hired some help so I wouldn't have spent so much time in the kitchen."

**Allow for alternative viewpoints.** Sophie said: "I realize that work comes first for you—after all it pays for everything—but I think you need to relax more." Philip said: "I know that you're not really interested in the money markets and that to outsiders it can easily get technical."

**Allow for the fact that you may be wrong.** Philip said: "Perhaps I was asking too much." Sophie said: "I could have made more of an effort."

**Look for a compromise.** Sophie said: "Perhaps we could have had them over to the house another time." Philip said: "Perhaps I could have booked them theater tickets instead and I could have enjoyed the family more."

## EXERCISE   ASSERTIVENESS QUIZ

Look at the following five scenarios and pick out the people-pleasing, the aggressive, and finally, the assertive response.

1. Your partner accepts an invitation to the party of a couple that you dislike. What is your reaction?

   a) List all the other times that she or he did not consult you.

   b) Suddenly remember a prior engagement that stops you attending.

   c) Listen to your partner's explanation, explain your misgivings, and agree to put in a quick appearance but not stay late.

2. Your partner is hanging over your shoulder, trying to attract your attention, while you are doing something that needs complete concentration. Do you …

   a) Ask if you could talk later.

   b) Tell him or her to back off.

   c) Stop and talk. It must be important?

3. You need time off work for something important but your supervisor says all the spaces on the vacation list are taken. What do you do?

   a) Go over your supervisor's head.

b) Clarify why it is important and ask for your supervisor's help finding a way round the problem.

c) Phone in sick on that day.

**4.** Your partner wants to try something a little spicy in the bedroom. What's your reaction?

a) Use the request as an opportunity to reevaluate your love life.

b) Accuse her or him of having an affair.

c) Feel guilty that you're not good enough and reluctantly go along with it.

**5.** Your partner is sulking or angry and complains: "You never do anything I want." Which is most likely to be your reply?

a) "I'm sorry but I do my best."

b) "Have you ever stopped to think why?"

c) "Never is putting it a bit strongly."

Congratulate yourself if you spotted the following:

Domineering—1a, 2b, 3a, 4b, 5b.

Passive—1b, 2c, 3c, 4c, 5a.

Assertive—1c, 2a, 3b, 4a, 5c.

Now go back over the questions and think which answer you would have given under those circumstances.

# THE RIGHT TO SAY NO

Returning to the basic rights from the beginning of the chapter, how do you reconcile your right to ask with your partner's right to refuse? First, you need to check that you are asking: "Would you ..." or "Could you ..." rather than giving an order: "Don't leave your clothes on the floor" or "Empty the washing machine." Next, make certain your partner has all the relevant information to fully assess your request. For example: "I am going to be home late, so would you mind ...?" These two strategies will significantly increase the chance of getting a "yes."

What if you need to say "no" to your partner? Remember you always have the right to refuse and it is often better to know that something is not possible—and make alternative arrangements—than be let down. More importantly, you are refusing the request, not the person. Next, use the ABC of communication:

A is for address the question: *I can't pick you up from work*

B is for bridge: *But, however, unfortunately, because,*

C is for communicate: *The car is going to be in the garage*

Finally, offer an alternative workable compromise. "Why don't we come home on the train together?" or "If you stay later at work, I could collect you when the car's ready."

# SOLVING A PROBLEM WITH ASSERTIVENESS

One of the benefits of being a couple where one partner is domineering and the other is passive is that—at least on the surface—it's easy and quick to make decisions. "We'll do it my way, fine, that's decided." When both partners' wants, needs, and beliefs are equally important, how do your resolve differences? I sum up the solution with this maxim:

**I can ask, you can say no, and we can negotiate.**

As you can imagine, this takes time but it is better to get all the issues up to the surface, achieve open and honest communication, and find a lasting solution. In the following chapters, I will look at how to negotiate and how to resolve any conflicts.

## SUMMING UP

We are not born assertive; it takes time to develop the ability to think through a problem and understand someone else's point of view. When we are under stress, we tend to act on gut reaction (learned as small children) rather than access our adult skills: explaining how we feel and think, in a direct, honest, appropriate, and spontaneous way. The good news is that these skills become easier with practice.

## IN A NUTSHELL:

- Think of your other half as a partner for problem-solving, not an opponent.

- What are the similarities, differences, and where do your goals dovetail? Look for a solution that is win/win.

- Never forget your and your partner have equal rights.

# CHAPTER SEVEN

# How to Argue Effectively

The assertive skills outlined in the last chapter assume that both parties can remain calm and rational. This is easier with work colleagues or friends whose behavior may hurt but seldom devastates us. When it comes to our partners, we might be assertive about minor matters—such as who's picking up the children—but what about the big issues? And what if we have fundamentally opposing opinions? In these circumstances, it is highly likely that the two of you will row. Remember, there is nothing wrong with a good argument. This is where both sides passionately hold an opinion, express it with consideration for the other person, listen to the opposing views, look for a solution, and make up afterward. What you don't want is a bad argument. This will involve name-calling, trying to win at all costs (even if it includes destroying your partner), not listening or walking away in the middle of a row, no solution, and a lingering nasty atmosphere. Although sometimes people think they have bad rows because their partner is a bad person, in my experience it is nearly always because someone is scared (so runs away or lashes out) or, more likely, does not know how to argue successfully.

# THREE STEPS FOR CONFLICT RESOLUTION

## 1. Explore: "I need to say ..."

This is all about explaining grievances and frustrations. Sometimes, one partner will need to do more venting. Don't try to reason; someone gripped by emotions will not have access to their rational mind. However, acknowledge their feelings: "I can see you are upset." Make certain all the feelings have been vented before moving on to the second step. Check with each other: "Do you need to say anything more."

**Tip:** Don't get personal. Rather than criticizing the person, complain about the behavior. Instead of "you're so untidy," try "Please do not leave your coffee cup on the counter."

## 2. Comprehending

Really hear each other out. Don't use the time your partner is talking to rehearse your defense—listen. Ask questions, so that you are clear what is meant and make certain that there are no misunderstandings. If you pay your partner the compliment of active listening, they will return the favor. If you are unable to listen, it probably means that you are still angry and need to vent some more.

**PART ONE: What is my responsibility?**

**Remembering that rows are "six of one and half a dozen of the other," think about your contribution.** How has your behavior extended or deepened the problem? When you have a clear idea of your own failings, find something—however small—and apologize for it.

For example, Nick and Anna, from Chapter Four, fought after their son's poor practice test results. Anna had been away on a training course and blamed Nick for not supervising his studying properly in her absence. The row went round and round in circles. Anna still felt annoyed, but apologized for her contribution to the friction: "I'm sorry that I gave you the silent treatment." A few hours later, and more reflection, Anna had another apology: "I was angry with our son too and I'm sorry I took some of it out on you."

**Tip:** Good questions start with "who," "what," "when," "where," but be careful with "why." These questions can sometimes sound like accusations rather than invitations to talk—so try softening the effect with "Have you any idea … why you feel angry" or "Could you explain … why you walked away."

**PART TWO: I comprehend your problems**

**Try to look at matters from your partner's viewpoint.** Are there any mitigating circumstances? What problems could she or he have been facing at the time? Is there anything from their past that makes this a blind spot? For example, Anna told Nick: "It must have been hard taking on both parental roles while I was away."

**Tip:** Sometimes when couples find it difficult to apologize for their contribution or find any mitigation for their partner, I ask them to change seats and literally imagine themselves in their partner's shoes. Five minutes arguing the other side is normally enough, but it is also an effective trick for understanding your partner's case better. Some couples change chairs at home, some cross over and argue from different corners of the room, and some make the switch just in their head. If you find it impossible to step into your partner's shoes, you are probably still too angry. In this case, return to exploring.

## 3. Action

Until you have both vented your feelings and both tried to comprehend each other's viewpoint, it is impossible to find a solution that will stick. Unfortunately, some couples try to move straight to action. As previously discussed, these shortcut solutions can work but generally leave one partner feeling resentful and therefore sow the seeds for future disputes.

When Nick and Anna truly understood each other's side of the row, Nick agreed to make supervising their son's schoolwork a greater priority, while Anna agreed that next time work took her away she'd try to get ahead of the laundry so Nick had more time to devote to their son. Ask yourself: "What have we learned from this fight?" "How will we do things differently next time?" "What should we do about this problem now?"

**Tip:** Don't be obsessed with winning. Either try to find a compromise, which pleases both parties, or aim for a trade off: "I won't read in bed if you give up the horrible habit of dunking cookies in your coffee." However, being aware of the sensitive areas, and an agreement to tread lightly, are often enough of an outcome.

## EXERCISE — WORKING THROUGH THE THREE STEPS TO CONFLICT RESOLUTION

Many couples want either to minimize disagreements or get over them as quickly as possible. Therefore, this exercise is designed to slow down your journey through the three steps.

1. Take three pieces of paper and mark one of these EXPLORE, another COMPREHEND, and the third one ACTION.

2. Take either a current dispute or an argument that you had recently.

3. Exploring is all about feelings—so each time one of you comes up with a feeling write it down on the EXPLORE page.

4. Exploring is also about opinions and beliefs: "A good father would look after his kids; a good wife would not go out in the evening." Write all this down too.

5. Exploring is about facts: "I can't get home before seven-fifteen." "Our household generates ten loads of laundry a week and someone needs to do it." Write down the most important ones.

**6.** Check back over your EXPLORE page. Make certain that along with the facts there are plenty of feeling words and beliefs. Can you think of anything more from either of these two categories?

**7.** Sometime a potential solution (for the ACTION sheet) might come up early in the conversation. Write the discovery on the relevant sheet, so it is not lost, but return to filling up the EXPLORE sheet.

**8.** Next, take the COMPREHEND sheet. Comprehending is about why things happen. For example: "I get angry because I'm stressed from work" or "I don't feel like sex when I'm ignored." Write these down.

**9.** Beliefs always come from somewhere: our upbringing, religion, general culture, or the media. The particularly powerful ones are from our childhood. How might your upbringing affect your beliefs? Write down your findings.

**10.** Looking at the EXPLORE and COMPREHEND pages, how can you use these insights to find a solution?

**11.** Solutions work best when there is a benefit for each party. For example, Partner A agrees to give Partner B five minutes' peace and quiet after arriving home, but in exchange Partner B agrees to give the children a bath later in the evening so A can rest. Make the tasks something that can be checked— as above—rather than general and hard to verify, such as "to try harder." Write the agreement on the ACTION page. You could even write it like a contract: "I agree to … if you agree to …" and both sign it.

**12.** A week later bring out the ACTION sheet and see if both of you have kept your side of the bargain. If you haven't, take three new pieces of paper write out the headings and go through the exercise again, exploring how both of you feel, comprehending what went wrong, and setting a better action plan.

# WHAT TYPE OF LISTENER ARE YOU?

There are two halves of an effective argument. The first is obvious: communicating our feelings, beliefs, and opinions. Sometimes, we think that if we can properly explain our viewpoint everything will be fine. However, many people overlook the second half of the equation. Unless we are a good listener, we will not understand our partner's viewpoint and, worse still, he or she will become more and more frustrated and less able to hear us. The result is a downward spiral of misinformation, misunderstanding, and misery.

There are three kinds of listening—argumentative, dismissive, and respectful—and although we can switch between them during an argument, most us of have a core style.

## Argumentative

While one partner is talking, the other is waiting to jump in, correct, or disagree. The result is lots of interruptions and the main issue can easily be lost in a maze of side arguments.

Amelia and Howard, both in their mid-thirties, had financial problems but rather than discussing how to solve them, would fight about particular purchases. "The flat-screen TV was a bargain, it was too good to miss, and anyway it will encourage us to stay in more and spend less," explained Howard. "Except it wasn't a good deal, was it?" Amelia interrupted. She had found the real price that he paid. "I also looked at several price comparison sites and you were had." Howard fought back by itemizing the cost of Amelia's recent meals out with friends.

In my experience, arguments about facts get couples nowhere. Firstly, this is because "facts" are always open to differing interpretation. Secondly, facts suggest right and wrong, a winner and a loser. Howard and Amelia were soon fighting about who was under the most stress and who contributed more to their marriage. However, they needed to work together if they were ever to solve their problems.

## Dismissive

Although the previous listening style is destructive, at least everything is out in the open. This second style is more internal and therefore harder to recognize. While one partner is talking, the other is putting mental brackets around some parts of the argument. This bracketing allows the listener to first play down the importance of the disputed sentence and then dismiss it altogether.

Jacob and Stephanie had been married for seven years and had a three-year-old child. They had a terrible fight after Stephanie phoned and asked Jacob to pick up some essential groceries on his way home but he had forgotten. "We live miles from the nearest store and it's a real trek," Stephanie explained. "I'd meant to get them. I had the best of intentions but my mind was too full of work," countered Jacob. When we deconstructed their argument, we found two rounds of bracketing. Firstly for Jacob, his good intentions allowed him to bracket Stephanie's frustration as unreasonable: "I really meant to go." For him, therefore, her anger was out of all proportion to the offense and he dismissed it. Meanwhile, Stephanie bracketed all Jacob's worry about a complex law case that he was wrapped up in: "He's always stressed by work, so there was nothing new." This allowed her to dismiss his mitigating circumstances.

The second round of dismissive listening came later that night. Jacob stormed out of the house and drove to the grocery store. When Stephanie tried to explain why she was so upset, Jacob closed down the conversation: "You've got your things. End of argument." He sighed and looked at me for support: "She got what she wanted and she's still angry." Stephanie turned to me: "I'm still angry because he just walked away mid argument." This is the cruelest form of dismissive listening.

## Respectful

When scientists watch newlywed couples argue, they can predict with 94 percent accuracy which couples will stay married and which will divorce. In some cases, they only need to listen for a few minutes. The key ingredient for a successful marriage is respectful listening. So I helped Stephanie and Jacob replay their argument and asked them to add as many respectful and supportive comments from the list below:

"You've got a good point."        "Tell me more."

"Yes, I see."        "I agree."

"So what you're saying is …"        "OK, so what do you suggest?"

"I can see how you feel."        "What do you think?"

"Right."        "How do you feel?"

"Go on."

These phrases show that although you might disagree, you are prepared to respect your partner's right to hold a different viewpoint. They are also a constant reminder that you might be arguing, but that you will survive, find a solution, and put it behind you. In addition, they lower the tension and stop the argument getting out of hand. So how did Stephanie and Jacob's argument replay with respectful listening?

"I was really angry that you forgot the groceries," said Stephanie.

"Go on," replied Jacob.

"Our daughter was refusing to get into the bath."

"So what you're saying is that you were at the end of your tether."

"I don't feel that I get enough support."

"I want to support you but you get so angry."

"You've got a good point," replied Stephanie, "It must drive people away."

"But I can see how you feel because I was angry at myself too. I really wanted to help but I let myself down."

Although stopping to look at my flip chart of respectful phrases felt a bit contrived, Stephanie and Jacob discovered more about each other than before and, more importantly, laid the foundations for a solution. Even better, after a couple of weeks, respectful listening became second nature and they found their own vocabulary.

## EXERCISE  IMPROVE YOUR COMMUNICATION

This is a fun game to play with your partner but it has a serious intention and will reveal a lot about how the two of you communicate.

- Sitting back to back, the first partner does a simple line drawing—like the ones below.

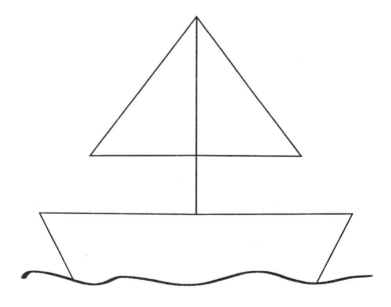

- The first partner does not show the second partner the picture but has to give instructions, so the second partner can draw it. For example, "Start at the top of the page, in the middle, and draw a straight line halfway down." You cannot describe the picture—"draw a flower"—but you can use geometric terms such as "draw a circle."

- The second partner can ask questions and check that they have heard the instructions correctly.

- Take as long as you like. It is not a race. Don't worry about being a good artist. This exercise is about communication.

- Keep your instructions short and to the point. Too much information, too quickly will lead to confusion.

- When you have finished, show each other your pictures and postmortem what helped make the picture an accurate copy and what hindered it.

- Swap over so both of you have a chance to describe a picture and a chance to follow the instructions and draw.

This is an exercise that I use in my workshops and it is interesting what people learn. Some "drawers" don't ask many questions and just assume that they are right. Some "drawers" are impatient and want to get on with the task and therefore miss vital information. Successful "drawers" keep checking that they have heard correctly: "Did you say a forty-five degree angle?" Some "describers" leave out vital bits of information, give contradictory instructions, or don't check that their partner has heard properly. What everybody learns is just how much time it takes to communicate effectively.

# FOUR PERSONAL PHILOSOPHIES FOR EFFECTIVE ARGUMENTS

So far in this chapter, we have looked at the shape of good argument and the importance of truly listening; the final ingredient is the right frame of mind.

## Look for the Good in the Other Person

Sometimes my female clients claim that their husbands are so bad at communicating feelings, and anger in particular, that it is impossible to argue effectively. I tend to shy away from gender stereotypes, partly because I have met plenty of emotionally articulate men and women who are not "in touch with their feelings," but mainly because of the "six of one and half a dozen of the other" rule (see Chapter One). Nearly every woman who complains about her partner using one of the anger avoidance strategies turns out to be using a complementary one herself. Sometimes it is easier to criticize our partner rather than understand our own contribution. This is why it is important to look for the good in your partner. If this feels difficult, try to understand how your partner arrived at his or her viewpoint. Eventually, you will move away from holding black and white positions and become aware of the gray in between.

## Be Flexible

Accept that there is no absolute truth about anything—only our own personal truths. Therefore, we should allow our partners to have a different view of our relationship—and not feel too challenged by it. After all, your partner is living with you, one experience; and you living with him or her, another experience. To explore the idea of being more flexible, make a list of all the things you need from a relationship (like trust, honesty, companionship) and all the things you would like. How many things on the need list are truly needs rather than preferences? Could something be transferred to the wish list? Finally, ask yourself: Am I asking too much from my partner? Could someone like a friend or even a professional provide this role? For example, some partners find it hard to sit with pain or grief. It might be desirable for your partner to be supportive and listen to complaints about your difficult mother or how much you miss your deceased father—but it might be asking too much.

## Be Optimistic

Optimistic people believe that there will be a good outcome from an argument. They will learn something important and find a resolution to a sticky problem. This allows them to avoid hopeless comments that turn a manageable row into a potential tragedy: "We'll never sort this out" or "If you feel like that I can't see the point carrying on." Better still, optimistic people put the problem down to something specific and transitory—"we've both been stressed lately"—and therefore feel better able to cope and search for a solution. By contrast, pessimists put problems down to something general and ingrained—"we're incompatible"—and therefore feel hopeless and overwhelmed. For help becoming more optimistic, see the final philosophy and the exercise at the end of this section.

## Accentuate the Positive

Generally it is easier to say what we don't want than to ask for what we do want. That's why, when trying to make things better with our partners, we end up either complaining or simply describing the problem.

So thinking of your complaints about your partner, write down the top three and turn them into positive requests: what you want rather than what you don't want. The more specific you can be the better.

**For example:**

Complaint: *You sulk to get your own way.*

Positive Request: *Please tell me outright when you disagree.*

How will I know when this has been achieved: *When we can happily go shopping together.*

Concrete Goal: *Let's choose the new faucets for the kitchen together.*

Complaint: *I'm always the driving force.*

Positive Request: *Don't leave all the decisions to me.*

How will I know when this has been achieved: *When my partner arranges a night out.*

Concrete Goal: *Actively planning a vacation together.*

## EXERCISE  ACCENTUATE THE POSITIVE

Look at these typical complaints and see if you could turn them into a positive and then find a request for a concrete but small goal. (Some possible answers can be found below.)

**1.** Why do I always have to clear up?

**2.** Will you stop mauling me?

**3.** You never initiate sex.

**4.** You're always hanging out with your friends.

**5.** I hate it when you avoid me.

**6.** You are way too critical.

**7.** Why can't you lighten up?

**8.** Why didn't you phone me?

**9.** You do nothing with the kids.

**10.** Isn't it about time you fixed the hall light?

**1.** Why do I always have to clear up?

**Positive:** I'm really grateful when you help me keep the house clean.

**Concrete Goal:** It would mean a lot to me if you emptied the trash.

**2.** Will you stop mauling me?

**Positive:** I like it when you stroke me gently.

**Concrete Goal:** Would you give me a soothing back massage?

**3.** You never initiate sex.

**Positive:** I loved it that time that you seduced me.

**Concrete Goal:** I'm going to back off asking and wait until you feel ready.

**4.** You're always hanging out with your friends.

**Positive:** I love our time together.

**Concrete Goal:** Shall we go to the movies on Wednesday?

**5.** I hate it when you avoid me.

**Positive:** It's great when you get home early.

**Concrete Goal:** Let's meet up after work and go for a drink together.

**6.** You are way too critical.

**Positive:** I really appreciated it when you complimented me about …

**Concrete Goal:** I think we should try to say thank you to each other more often.

**7.** Why can't you lighten up?

**Positive:** I really enjoy our fun times together.

**Concrete Goal:** Let's do something great this weekend.

**8.** Why didn't you phone me?

**Positive:** It's so nice to hear your voice during the day.

**Concrete Goal:** Let's try to touch base with each other sometime tomorrow.

**9.** You do nothing with the kids.

**Positive:** It means so much to the kids when you do things with them.

**Concrete Goal:** Could you take the kids to the park this afternoon?

**10.** Isn't it about time you fixed the hall light?

**Positive:** Thank you so much for fixing the sticky drawer, it's made my life so much easier.

**Concrete Goal:** Do you think you'll be able to fix the hall light this weekend?

# WHAT IF THE ARGUMENT TURNS DESTRUCTIVE?

Even with the best will in the world, sometimes a productive argument can go off the rails, but don't panic. Remember, it is better to have a bad argument than none at all.

- When the temperature rises, this is usually a sign that the real feelings are beginning to come to the surface and a sign of hope. In counseling, the arguments get worse before they get better.

- Resist the temptation to say "and another thing" and throw in additional gripes. These examples might strengthen your case, but they also prolong and complicate the argument. Instead, try to solve one issue at a time.

- Have you been criticizing rather complaining? In general, complaints use "I" while criticism uses "You." For example, a complaint would be: "I wanted us to go to bed at the same time." While as a criticism: "You didn't come to bed on time." The first invites a discussion about bedtimes, the second will make your partner defensive and prolong an argument.

- Shouting and getting passionate are acceptable. But if the language gets abusive or there is even a threat of pushing or slapping, you should separate for ten to fifteen minutes and return when both of you have cooled down. Whoever feels threatened should call "time-out." This means separating to different rooms or allowing one another to go out for a short walk or drive. The exact length of time apart is up to each couple but should be negotiated beforehand. It is vital that discussion is resumed—some couples have a quick postmortem and others enter round two—otherwise the person in the middle of a vent will be unwilling to let their partner have time-out for fear of not getting an opportunity to properly release.

- Remember the Eighty/Twenty rule (Chapter One) and look at what might be lying underneath the arguments that keep returning and returning, and returning. One couple, in counseling, fought about defrosting the freezer. She felt that he bought too many frozen products without using up what was already there. He did the cooking and felt it was up to him to plan the meals. It got very nasty, especially as her parents had given them lots of chicken, which he claimed took up most of the space. This battle kept on recurring, with variations, for several weeks and still the freezer had not been defrosted. Finally, we looked deeper and found the core issue. The wife had bought the freezer before he moved in, and felt that he did not respect her property. In her opinion, if the freezer was not properly maintained it would break down and they couldn't afford a new one. Her husband had a more "come what may" approach to money and generally felt that they would muddle through. When he truly understood his partner's fears, the issue disappeared and the freezer was finally defrosted.

🌢 Use the Three Steps to Conflict Resolution Exercise (see page 110) to postmortem your argument. A good opening gambit would be to apologize for your half of the argument. Next look at what went wrong. A good way to achieve this, without reigniting the row, would be to say something like: "I don't want to bring up the issues again, but why do you think it got out of hand?" "How could we have approached it differently?" "What can we learn?"

## SUMMING UP

If arguments go round in circles it is often because one of the three stages of conflict resolution—explore, comprehend, action—have been skipped. Arguing and properly making up again is the most intense form of bonding you can have. Isn't it about time to prove how much you love your partner by having a really good argument?

## IN A NUTSHELL:

- Express yourself in simple and short sentences, and concentrate on one idea at a time. Your partner will only be able to absorb so much information.

- Better communication starts with better listening. You do not have to agree with your partner, but at least look through their eyes and understand.

- Think about how you can turn your complaints into positive requests.

# CHAPTER EIGHT

———

# Think Smarter

I f we're honest, we can all name areas of our relationship that we'd like to improve. Perhaps your partner uses Saturday as a chance to pursue a favorite hobby while you'd prefer to spend the time together. Maybe you've fallen out over your partner's reluctance to share the cooking or you've given up trying to keep track of your finances because he or she loses all the receipts. It does not matter if it is something petty—such as the best place to keep the garbage bags—or something as important as which school your children should attend, these long-running disputes about family, household management, and social life can really grind down your relationship.

Unfortunately, the most common ways of dealing with them—such as complaining, nagging, sulking, blackmailing, playing martyr, or agreeing to one thing but doing another—are not only unpleasant and ineffective in the long term, but also exacerbate the problem. In the worst cases, couples end up having arguments about arguments. However, there is a new strategy that not only takes the heat out of long-running disputes, but can actually solve them too. It is called nudging.

Surprisingly, the idea comes originally from politics. Governments have realized that lecturing and legislating—even if it is something that we know is in our best interests, such as drinking less or putting money aside for our old age—not only puts our backs up but makes us dig in our heels and become more committed to our harmful habits. This is why the book *Nudge: Improving Decisions about Health, Wealth and Unhappiness* (Yale University Press, 2008) by Richard H. Thaler and Cass R. Sunstein—two professors from Chicago University—has attracted a lot of interest.

Thaler and Sunstein call the concept "Libertarian Paternalism." Libertarian because people should be free to do what they wish. Paternalism because it is legitimate for governments to influence people's behavior to make their lives longer, healthier, and better. They write: "To count as a mere nudge, the intervention must be easy and cheap to avoid. Nudges are not mandates." Therefore a school canteen putting fruit at eye level—where pupils are more likely to see and buy it—is a nudge; banning junk food is not.

As a marital therapist, I am used to helping couples who are stuck in the same demand/withdraw cycle as politicians. So I wondered: what would happen if my clients nudged rather cajoled, tricked, or bullied each other into submission?

# HARNESS THE POWER OF THE NUDGE

I have adapted the concepts that underlie Libertarian Paternalism into four interlocking strategies. Which ones would work for you?

## Choice Architecture

**What's the big idea?** This is the person who organizes the context in which others make decisions. It could be a doctor describing different possible treatments or a grocery store manager who decides where stock is displayed in the store. Although we like to think these people are being neutral, they are making hundreds of small decisions that have a major impact on our behavior. For example, the grocery store could put the healthiest options in the prime positions, or the items that generate the most profit. The doctor could marshal the statistics so patients elect for his or her OWN field of speciality.

**Put it into action:** Overall, relationships aim to be fifty/fifty but there are places where each partner is in charge. Naomi and Barry have been married for fifteen years and over that time have established clear roles. Naomi, for example, was responsible for organizing their social life but would often end up doing activities she was not particularly keen on. So how could she nudge rather than dictate to Barry? First, we looked at how she described the options for the weekend. Research shows that the first name on a ballot paper and the first special described by a waiter do the best. Next, we cut back the number of possibilities so she did not overwhelm Barry with choice and allow him to fall back on the same old choices—such as "taking it as it comes." Finally, Naomi accepted that she was the choice architect and edited out the options that appealed to her less. "Over the long weekend, I suggested we visited my parents who had hired an apartment by the sea or went to a concert and firework spectacular in the park. Previously, I might have added just hanging out at the local wine bar. Much to my surprise, he happily went to the concert and enjoyed it." Barry was still free to choose—rather than be forced into going—but Naomi had nudged him away from the wine bar.

**Warning:** Don't overstretch yourself and try to become the choice architect in areas where you have no control—such as what time your partner leaves work.

## Resetting the Default

**What's the big idea?** Although economists think of us as rational, weighing up all the options, and making informed choices, we are often lazy, inconsistent, fail to act in our own self-interest, and stick with the status quo. Companies understand this inertia and profit from it. For example, a subscription TV channel will offer a free trial offer but set up a default where you are automatically subscribed unless you cancel. Their retention rate is much higher than if the default is that customers have to opt in.

**Put it into action:** In contentious issues around the house, look at the default position. Both Sheena and John were, in theory, responsible for laundry, but when the basket was overflowing the default was that

Sheena would curse and set to. "I don't generally mind but I just wish he'd help when I'm really stressed," she explained. However, she had underestimated the power of inertia: John would mean to help but would fall back into his usual evening routine of fixing a drink and settling down to watch television.

Instead of Sheena playing the martyr or bitching about the laundry, we arranged a nudge for John by setting a new more equitable default system: Whoever came home first would automatically put on a load of washing. If Sheena was working late, this would invariably be John and instead of being "a favor," it became part of the relationship status quo.

**Warning:** Don't expect your partner to settle into the new routine straightaway; it takes time to build up a helpful habit. So be patient and, if needed, add in the other strategies.

## Framing the Options

**What's the big idea?** How you inform people has a big effect on their behavior. In the Petrified Forest National Park in Arizona, they needed to stop visitors taking souvenir samples home. In an experiment, they changed the signs every two hours between a negative message stressing the harm done by stealing pieces of petrified wood and a positive one asking for help to protect the forest. The positive were significantly more effective than the negative ones.

**Put it into action:** Instead of telling your partner to do something, you can nudge by framing a possible window of opportunity. Ryan had fallen out with his teenage daughter after some clumsy remark about her weight. His wife, Mina, tried to patch things up but Ryan really need to talk to his daughter himself. Unfortunately, he kept putting off a possibly nasty confrontation.

After discussing the nudge concept, Mina enabled the discussion by telling him: "I'm going to be out this afternoon, so the two of you will be alone." As Ryan later explained: "This planted the seed in my mind and helped me to psyche myself up."

**Warning:** Do not fall into the trap of introducing something in a negative way: "I know you're not going to want to ..." as they most probably will agree with you.

## Incentives and Feedback

**What's the big idea?** In California, householders were informed if they were below or above average in their energy consumption. Heavy users began to cut back and the positive effect was magnified when the energy company added a happy smiley symbol to bills heading in the right direction. Local authorities, such as Tayside in Scotland, have been encouraging smokers to quit in return for grocery vouchers.

**Put it into action:** People underestimate the power of incentives because this strategy has failed them in the past. In most cases, they were not aware of the other elements of a successful nudge. Perhaps they have not targeted areas where they are truly the choice architect and had such poor default systems that they had to give countless incentives or praise and ended up devaluing them. However, if you have followed the other nudge strategies, even small rewards will have a big impact.

When giving positive feedback, thank your partner at the time but reinforce the message by communicating your appreciation a few days later too. This will make your praise seem more considered and not just a reflex action.

**Warning:** Don't bribe your partner as this will make you resentful in the long term, and don't give false praise as this ultimately puts your partner's back up.

## IT'S A NUDGE RATHER THAN A SHOVE WHEN ...

1. You can defend your actions in public–otherwise it is sneaky manipulation.

2. Your partner has the freedom to opt out–otherwise it is an order.

3. You are up for your partner nudging you back–otherwise you are just being a control freak!

# TWO WAYS OF THINKING

Psychologists and neuroscientists have begun to agree on how our brains function: we think in two completely different ways. The first is called "Automatic" and happens so quickly and instinctively that we don't even associate it with thinking—such as ducking when a ball is thrown in our direction or smiling at a kitten walking across a piano keyboard. Neuroscientists believe the Automatic System is associated with the oldest parts of the brain, inherited from our reptile ancestors. The second form of thinking is called "Reflective" and is rational and self-conscious. The best way to explain the difference is that we use our Automatic System when speaking our mother tongue but our Reflective System when learning and speaking a foreign language. The following table explains more:

| AUTOMATIC SYSTEM | REFLECTIVE SYSTEM |
| --- | --- |
| Gut reaction | Head |
| Uncontrolled | Controlled |
| Effortless | Effortful |
| Instinctive | Deductive |
| Fast | Slow |
| Unconscious | Self-aware |
| Trained by repetition | Open to rational argument |

In many ways, we are open to nudges because they work on our Automatic System where we respond instinctively, rather than weighing up the options with our Reflective System.

## The Downside of Automatic Thinking

We lead busy and complicated lives and don't have the time or the energy to analyze everything. Therefore we use lots of shortcuts to process information quickly. For example, we rely on rules of thumb to work out the cost of something in a foreign currency—and get a shock when we finally receive our credit card statements—or stereotypes to guide our response to people (the elderly are frail or young people are open to new ideas) where a moment's thought tells us that such sweeping generalizations are meaningless. In other words, we might unquestioningly rely on our Automatic System, but it frequently lets us down.

When it comes to dealing with our partner, we underplay the importance of Automatic Thinking and overestimate the power of Reflective Thinking—especially when we're trying to change long-held prejudices. For example, Ashley had a hard time recovering from her husband's affair with a work colleague. "Although Wyatt doesn't see her on a day-to-day basis, they come together on major projects like pitching new work to clients," she explained. "He'd agreed to let me know whenever they would be contact but time after time, he's let me down." The most recent occasion had been only a few days previously. "I'd had a bad day and phoned Wyatt to let off steam but he seemed very distant and I knew something was wrong," said Ashley. "But I told you the truth when I got home," said Wyatt. He had been in the car with his former affair partner. "When the boss suggested that I give her a lift, I couldn't really say no."

"You could have sent me a text so I'd have known and I certainly wouldn't have poured out my heart when that woman could have overheard."

"This is why I don't always tell. My only reward for being honest is grief, drama, and a cold shoulder in bed."

Ashley thought this was unfair. She could list lots of times when Wyatt had told her about some contact and she'd just thanked him. Unfortunately, Wyatt's Automatic System—trained by repetition—expected a bad reaction. His Reflective System might have been able to recall the positive occasions, but the bad ones—because of their severity—had registered much stronger and deeper into his brain.

**How to use this knowledge:** Learn the importance of repeating your positive new behavior and don't be disappointed if it takes a while for your partner to respond and for the Reflective System to take over from the Automatic.

## The Downside of Reflective Thinking

Our rational brain values words over everything else. If we can just make our case effectively and logically, we must be persuasive. However, communication is made up of much more than just words. Professor Albert Mehrabian of the University of California did some groundbreaking work in the Sixties about how we communicate feelings and attitude. For face-to-face communication, he found that we used three main ways:

1. WORDS. Those we actually use when speaking.

2. MUSIC. The tone of voice, pace, pitch, and volume.

3. DANCE. Our body language.

If these three components had to add up to 100 percent of communication, how much in percentage terms do you think WORDS make up? Have a guess. (The answer is below, upside down.)

Jane and Christopher, from Chapter Three, had had a nasty row after he stopped in the middle of their lovemaking because he felt she was just going through the motions. "I don't want her to do it just for me," said Christopher. "How do you think that makes me feel? I want her to be an equal partner."

Words 7% Music 38%, and Dance 55%

"I kept telling you: I want to sort this problem out just as much as you," Jane snapped back at him.

I stopped her: "What sort of message do you think you're giving Christopher?"

"That I want to sort out our problems?" Jane looked puzzled.

Using Reflective Thinking, she had imagined that her words alone had counted. However the MUSIC and DANCE had been completely different. Her tone had been far from conciliatory—she almost spat the words out. Her body language had also been aggressive—she had leaned forward and her eyes were flashing with anger. This had been what Christopher had responded to.

**How to use this knowledge:** Make certain that your words, tone, and body language match. If there is a difference between what you're saying and how you're acting, the other person is more likely to believe the MUSIC and DANCE than the WORDS. In most cases, it is better to tell your partner just how upset you feel—rather than let this knowledge leak out through your tone and body language. Once you've calmed down a little, then you can try to build a bridge with words—but not before.

## EXERCISE  PRIMING

This exercise combines both ways of thinking. It will not only influence your partners' Automatic System, but encourage him or her to engage their Reflective System too.

**1.** Researchers have discovered that just asking people if they intend to do something actually increases the likelihood that they will. For example, being asked if you will vote increases the chance of voting by 25 percent and being asked if you plan to buy a new car increases the likelihood by 35 percent. In effect, just mentioning behavior gives a nudge in that direction.

**2.** So prime your partner's Automatic System by asking: "When can you …?" "Have you any idea when you will be able to …?" (For example, cut back the hedge or speak to your mother about babysitting.)

**3.** Make certain that your body language is relaxed or neutral. If you're exasperated, your message will come across as "Isn't it about time that you …." In these circumstances, it is better to choose another occasion or your attempt to prime will be interpreted as nagging.

**4.** Encourage your partner to engage his or her Reflective System by asking: "Is there anything that I can do to help?" This will allow him or her to consider possible obstacles and think through the best to tackle the task: "It would help if you could collect the children from swimming so I could get an early start on the hedge" or "I'm really busy, would you mind phoning my mother?"

**In action:** Mike and Hannah would argue about renovating their Colonial house. "He will have agreed to finish sanding the floor but it's always 'just let me finish this beer' or 'I'm watching this crucial baseball game,'" explains Hannah. "We end up having terrible rows because I keep tripping over the equipment. Surely, he can just get on and do it and then watch television?"

Her partner, Mike, would have every intention of sanding the floor but be sidetracked by momentary pleasures, and soon it would be too late to start. The situation had deteriorated to such a point that Hannah thought "He doesn't care about my feelings" and Mike thought Hannah was "unreasonable."

Instead of getting angry, I helped Hannah to prime Mike by asking: "Are you going to work on the floor this weekend?" and follow up with "Are you going to ask your brother for help?"

However, don't get carried away with priming, to the point that your partner pictures an order with deadlines and penalty clauses, and be flexible enough so that your partner can set his or her own timetable.

# NEGOTIATING

With a better understanding of how we think and how we make decisions, it is time to look at what happens when our partner wants one thing and we want another. Is it possible to nudge him or her toward our way of thinking?

We spend a lot of time negotiating with our partner. Which restaurant will we eat at? Which movie shall we see? What time should our daughter be back home? Unfortunately, just doing something frequently doesn't necessarily make us any good at it. Especially as when the discussion goes seamlessly, we are not really aware what helped us reach agreement and when it goes wrong, we are angry, frustrated, or resentful toward our partner and not in the mood to explore our mistakes. So, for many people, negotiating is a bit of a mystery.

There are, in effect, two types of negotiating. The first is called Opposing and is competitive. Each side tries to get as close to their preferred outcome as possible. A classic example would be going into a car salesroom; you want the lowest price and the best benefits while the owner wants to make the largest profit. The second is called Cooperative and the main focus is reaching a mutually beneficial agreement. For example, the management needs to make savings—or the company will no longer be financially viable—but the union wants to protect jobs.

So how do these two types of negotiating work when dealing with your partner?

## Opposing

This style of negotiating can easily go wrong:

Each partner takes up an extreme position

↓

One partner offers a tiny concession

↓

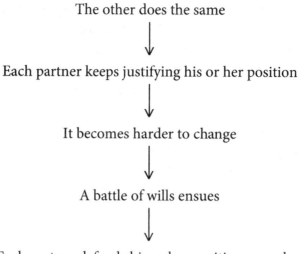

The other does the same

↓

Each partner keeps justifying his or her position

↓

It becomes harder to change

↓

A battle of wills ensues

↓

Each partner defends his or her position or makes
an even smaller concession to keep the negotiations alive

↓

Each partner becomes more stubborn and focused on his
or her position, not what is good for the relationship

↓

**Result** = No agreement or a poor one.

**In action:** Lucas and Sarah had been married for seven years and had two small children. Lucas' passion in life was playing golf. In fact, he had wanted to be a professional but things hadn't worked out and he had taken an office job. "I don't begrudge Lucas his golf," said Sarah, "I know he needs to unwind but it really eats into family time."

Both partners had taken an extreme position before coming into counseling. Lucas wanted to be able to play on some Sundays: "There's a couple of competitions that are being run at the club and I'd like to take part." Sarah was horrified: "I'm not that keen on you playing every Saturday, but Sundays too? We wouldn't see you at all. Couldn't we have just one or two golf-free weekends for a change?"

Lucas offered a small concession: "I could go earlier and that way I'd be back for lunch and we'd still have the afternoon."

However, both Lucas and Sarah kept justifying their positions: "I work really hard and this is my one bit of fun," he said. "The children are small and they want to do things with us at the moment," she countered.

Next, they started defending their positions:

"I let you go away on that golfing weekend," said Sarah.

"It was my brother's stag do; I could hardly tell them 'my wife won't let me come,'" Lucas replied.

Sarah was back on the attack: "So you waited for the last possible moment to tell me—although you'd known for months."

Lucas replied: "Do you wonder with the amount of grief that I get?"

The subject became so toxic that we stopped discussing golf in their counseling sessions and focused on less controversial issues.

## Cooperative

While in opposing negotiations your partner is part of the problem, with cooperative negotiations she or he is part of the solution:

Neither party puts a request on the table
but instead discusses the issue at hand

↓

Each party explains their interests and needs

↓

Both listen with respect whether they agree or not

↓

They look for common and shared interests

$\downarrow$

Many possible approaches are discussed

$\downarrow$

Each party focuses on finding a solution
rather than promoting their favored position

$\downarrow$

**Result** = Agreement

**In action:** Further into counseling, Lucas and Sarah tried to discuss golf again, but instead of restating their positions, they talked about weekends together that had been a success. "I enjoy going places with you and the kids," said Lucas, "we've had some lovely days out." Sarah agreed that things had been much better: "I haven't minded so much about the golf—especially since you've been going earlier—and I've been able to get on with the chores."

Next, they explained their interests. "Golf is important to me but so is my family," said Lucas. "That's why I work so hard to pay for nice things." "I want you to be happy and I do appreciate everything that you do for us," Sarah replied, "but I want you to get the best out of our children."

From this position, it was not difficult to find some common goals: being good parents, enjoying family trips, each needing their own time.

They discussed Sarah having a night to play sport during the week and how Lucas could use that night to catch up with his paperwork—rather than Sunday nights.

Ultimately, they made no hard and fast deal. Lucas did play in competitions—which occasionally meant golfing both Saturday and Sunday. However, he made up for it by skipping golf one weekend and taking the whole family camping instead. He also started taking odd days off during the school vacations for family trips rather than just reserving them for golf. By using cooperative negotiation, they could deal with each golfing case on its own merits.

# EXERCISE NEGOTIATING TIPS

It is often easier to introduce Cooperative negotiating when the stakes are low, so either practice at work or find an uncontroversial topic with your partner.

- Indicate clearly your needs and interests.

- Remember the old saying: "If you don't ask, you don't get."

- Listen carefully to the other person, repeat back their position so you can be clear that you've fully understood.

- Just because the other person asks for something doesn't mean you necessarily have to give it.

- Look for common ground.

- People prefer to buy than be sold to. By this I mean we like to choose rather than have a particular option rammed down our throat.

- Stress your desire to reach agreement. For example, "I'm confident that we can find something that will work for both of us" or "We're not that far apart."

- Remind each other of what you agree about—if only in principle at this stage.

- Leave something in reserve—especially in business dealings—so that you have a way of closing the deal.

- When you've reached agreement, repeat what you're going to do. This is partly because it ensures there are no misunderstandings but it also reminds both parties what has been achieved.

## SUMMING UP

Nudging takes into consideration how people behave in the real world rather than how we'd like to believe they do. We are influenced by lots of seemingly insignificant decisions and decide on a course of action as much emotionally as rationally. This is why words alone are never enough to convince our partner's about contentious issues—especially if our words are at odds with the tone of our voice or our body language.

## IN A NUTSHELL:

- If you slip into a competitive style of negotiating, you are probably too focused on your own needs. If you are too quick to accommodate, you are too focused on your partners needs. However, when you're compromising, you are aware of both of your needs.

- If negotiations become fraught, tell your partner how you're feeling–even if it is angry or frustrated–rather than suppressing your emotions. This helps your partner understand the effect his or her actions are having on you.

- Don't shut down any solution–however off-the-wall or impractical–because discussing it can easily lead to a great suggestion.

# CHAPTER NINE

## Carrots Rather Than Sticks

So far my love hacks have been aimed at couples who are in a relatively good place but want to improve their communication, resolve long-standing issues, or protect their love from the everyday stresses of raising a family and paying the bills. But what if your problems are more ingrained, you have been unhappy for a long time, and feel only a revolution will solve your problems? What if your partner is either happy enough with the status quo or in denial about the extent of your misery? The love hacks in the following chapters are aimed at dealing with a crisis.

One of the oldest debates is which works best: the carrot or the stick? Marcial Losada, an organizational psychologist from Michigan, decided to test this proposition. He observed businesses and on the basis of results, customer satisfaction, and opinions of managers and peers he divided the staff into high, mid, and low performers. Losada found that the high-performance divisions used up to five times as many positive comments (carrots) than negative one (sticks). In sharp contrast, the poor performing teams gave significantly more negative statements than positive.

John Gottman, emeritus professor at the University of Washington has studied how couples interact for over thirty years and claims to be able to predict with 90 percent accuracy which newlyweds will remain married and which will divorce four to six years later. He stresses the importance of positive strokes too, such as compliments, thank yous, reassurances, recognition of the other's viewpoints. We imagine that one unpleasant gesture—such as criticism or complaint—can be canceled out by one positive stroke. However, Gottman's findings suggest that our instincts are wrong. Couples that stay married will balance one negative with five positives, while couples that divorce can often have ten negatives to one positive.

With all the research pointing to five carrots to one stick as the optimum balance, how do you achieve this goal? Increasing the ratio of positives does not mean becoming unbearably cheerful or making up compliments—as this can come across as false. Instead, focus on communicating more effectively. Most people feel hundreds of positive emotions about their friends and work colleagues every day: "It's nice to see you" or "I really admire the way that you handled that." Unfortunately, we keep most of these thoughts to ourselves. So try an experiment and tell your partner about these private positives. After seven days, stop and assess the atmosphere at home:

🌷 How has it improved?

🌷 Is your partner more willing to cooperate?

🌷 How do you feel?

## EXERCISE SO HOW DO YOU COME ACROSS AS POSITIVE?

- **Smile.** This will not only make you seem warm but approachable too.

- **Maintain good eye contact.** People who cannot look us directly in the eye are considered to be lying or trying to hide something.

- **Think positive thoughts.** We like people who make us feel good about the world and, most important of all, about ourselves. Someone who criticizes, even if it is just something inconsequential like the decor, might be perceived as clever, intelligent, or funny but we are always wary. Deep down, we fear they will be equally cutting about us behind our backs or, worse still, that the criticism is an indirect attack on our tastes or our personality.

- **Appear interested.** Repeat back key phrases so the person speaking knows you have been listening ("So he stepped right out in front of you") and, most powerful of all, identifying feeling ("You must have been horrified").

# START WITH SMALL CARROTS

Although the love hacks in this section of the book are focused on making bigger changes, it is still important to lay the groundwork first. Here are two small but positive strategies for getting your partner to open up and allow you to understand her or him better.

## Encouraging Body Language

- Leaning slightly toward someone—although not too close so that their personal space is invaded—shows interest.

- Crossing your arms will make you look defensive, so keep an open posture.

- Nodding signals not just encouragement but demonstrates involvement in the story that you're being told. However, be aware that we normally nod in pairs. Three nods suggests that you wish to interrupt.

- Blinking can also set a romantic mood. We blink every two or three seconds and increasing the rate will increase your partner's too. Conversely, slowing down a blink to a third of its natural speed can be sexually attractive as it mimics a wink.

- Mirroring—where you match your body posture to someone else's—can amplify any intimacy that is growing between two people.

- Babies love the game "peek-a-boo"—where you hide your face behind your hand and then suddenly appear from nowhere. They will play it over and over without ever seeming to get bored. Adults who are interested in each other play a very similar game: looking at someone, then looking away and back again. They also use props such as menus to disappear behind and then suddenly appear.

•

## Encouraging Easy, Flowing Conversation

- Value small talk. It is a good way of warming up for a more interesting conversation and provides a breathing space to relax and unwind after a tough day. So make a mental note of opening subjects that are noncontroversial. For example: weather, recent news story, celebrity goings-on, and television programs.

- The secret of good conversation is to offer small snippets of self-disclosure. Don't just say that you've had a busy day—talk about a particular project or what your son or daughter have been doing.

- Look for areas of conversational connection. What might interest your partner? What could prompt him or her to ask questions?

- Echo your partner's language. If he is a teacher and calls his pupils' "kids" use the same word as this will help increase your connection. If she is a businesswoman and refers to her "firm," don't subsequently call it a "company" as this will put up a conversational barrier.

- Don't block topics. You might not be particularly interested in the new out of town shopping mall or the community garden, but listening attentively shows that you value your partner and consider her or his activities interesting.

144

🌱 Never underestimate the importance of asking questions. Everybody likes talking about themselves and their interests. A good listener will always be appreciated. So as well as offering your snippets of self-disclosure, be ready to take up your partner's too.

🌱 Once you and your partner are talking freely about day-to-day news and can bring up day-to-day issues, it is much easier to move onto significant problems or unburden your heart.

## BIGGER CARROTS

It is human nature to repay favors. Across all cultures, and throughout history, doing something for someone else effectively puts them in our debt and encourages them to return the favor as soon as possible.

A good example is a classic experiment carried out by Dr. Dennis Regan from Cornell University who gathered volunteers supposedly to measure art appreciation in teams of two. Unknown to the volunteers, their partner for the test was his assistant. Halfway through, the assistant would explain that he was thirsty and ask to go off and buy a can of soda. On some occasions, he would return with a second can for his partner too. After the test had finished, the assistant announced that he was selling raffle tickets for charity. The teammates who had been given the can of soda were twice as likely to buy tickets—even though they cost much more than the price of drink.

This idea of reciprocity was also studied by Francis Flynn, who we met earlier, from Stanford University. The staff at an airline customer service desk were allowed to swap shifts and this allowed Flynn to look at favors in the real world rather than an artificial situation in the laboratory. Her work found a significant difference between the recipient of the favor and the person doing the favor. The recipient valued the favor the most immediately afterward. Over time, the benefits—for example, being able to attend your child's school play—recede into a distant memory and became less valuable. Conversely, the favor-doer placed a low value on agreeing to cover the shift at the time—"no problem"—but gives a greater value to the favor as time passes.

This research demonstrates the gulf that opens when there is no opportunity to return the favor within a reasonable time frame. While the recipient has possibly forgotten the incident, the favor-doer is left holding a growing grudge.

So how can you use this research?

- **Understand the importance of favors.** Although, in theory, we do things for love, marriage and long-term relationships are effectively a complex web of favors given and returned.

- **Understand the nature of favors.** A favor is a one-off kindness. When something becomes a regular occurrence, it will slide from a favor into an entitlement. So although cooking your partner's favorite meal is a nice thing to do—and would definitely count as a carrot—it is unlikely to be a favor (unless cooking is normally your partner's responsibility).

- **Reciprocate as soon as possible.** If your partner does not ask for a favor, offer to go that extra mile for him or her. For example: "Would you like me to collect you from your girl's night so you don't have to bother about finding a taxi?" or "I'll take your mother to the hospital so that you can go to golf."

- **Keep the favors at a sensible size.** With the reciprocal nature of favors, we feel overwhelmed if our partner does something too big and fear it is impossible to repay.

- **Understand that favors in the rear-view mirror can seem bigger.** This is another reason to keep favors to manageable proportions as your partner will be most grateful at the time, but you will value the favor more over time and could become resentful. (The following story illustrates this point.)

When Brady and Maya came into counseling, the air was thick with distrust and resentment. So I investigated what Brady had done for Maya and vice versa.

"My aunt died two years ago and left me a significant amount of money," said Brady, "but as things were not that good between us, I thought I'd throw a big surprise fortieth birthday party for Maya." He also bought her an extravagant present. In his mind, these favors meant the end of getting "grief" from his wife.

Maya saw things differently: "I'm not saying that I didn't enjoy the party. It was wonderful, but if you'd discussed it with me, I'd much rather we'd spent the money on something practical—such as new windows for the house." In effect, Brady's favor to Maya—in the rearview mirror—still appeared big to him but to her it appeared so small, it was invisible (unless she was reminded).

Suddenly, in the counseling room, Maya became angry:

"If you were trying to buy me with that jewelry, you can take it back to the store right away."

"It was a present. Don't be stupid," he replied.

This dispute underlines the importance of small and medium sized, rather than big carrots. Nobody wants to feel bought or in debt.

## EXERCISE  CARROTS AND STICKS IN ACTION

Getting your partner to say "yes" is all about finding the appropriate carrots, but that doesn't mean there isn't a place for an occasional small stick:

1. **Instead of criticizing what you don't like, praise what you do like.** When training my first puppy, Flash, I would much rather he did his "business" on the open fields behind our house than on the streets where I would have to pick up after him. So if he went on the grass verge, I would make him sit while I got out a bag. If he waited an extra five minutes and went under a hedgerow, I would offer lots of praise. Within a few weeks, he always went in the countryside.

2. **Keep reinforcing good behavior.** When my puppy stole a shoe and ran round the house with it, I'd ignore him so he quickly tired of that game. If he took a snooze in the sun at the top of the stairs, I would quietly praise and stroke him. In this way, I rewarded the quiet behavior that allowed me to get on with my writing and did not fall into the trap of rewarding bad behavior with negative attention. It might take a while for your partner to put his or her coffee cup in the dishwasher but make a point of saying "Thank you, I really appreciated that" rather ignoring him or her or saying something sarcastic.

3. **Make your intervention timely.** Dogs live in the moment, so if you find a chewed shoe—even if you put it under their nose—they cannot associate the telling off with their action. In the dog's mind, he has been lying down quietly, minding his own business, and for some unknown reason he's in trouble. However if you catch him with the shoe in his mouth, this is the perfect time to say "no." Humans have a better sense of time than dogs, but getting upset about something that happened weeks ago is pointless and in the same way, praising the behavior that you like is more powerful in the moment too.

4. **Small reprimands can work.** When Flash was still young, I took him to my writers group. After lunch, I walked him round and round the nearby park, giving him his instruction to empty his bladder—without success. I took him round my friend's backyard, still no luck. Finally, I gave up and returned inside. Two minutes later, he squatted down in her living room and relieved himself. Without thinking, I took him by the scruff of the neck, shook him like a bitch would discipline her puppies, and then placed him outside. He never repeated this behavior in my house or anybody else's. The intervention worked because the punishment was small, timely, and over quickly. Small sticks that will work with your partner might include a disapproving look or a complaint (please don't ...).

# APPRECIATIVE INQUIRY

The regular way to solve a problem is to look at what has gone wrong and to seek a solution. However, in the 1980s, businesses, which wanted to change and renew, started to embrace an idea called Appreciative Inquiry (AI). Rather than fixing problem areas, AI focuses on building on what already works. AI practitioners believe this approach makes staff more creative, increases trust, and brings out the basic goodness in people. By contrast, problem solving just encourages blame and faultfinding.

Recently, I have started using these techniques with clients who are stuck in a rut because it fitted with my philosophy that carrots work better than sticks. But before I explain how you can use AI, let's look at how it works in the business setting.

Every intervention has to fulfill four criteria:

**Appreciative:** What assets does a company have? What does it do well?

**Applicable:** Staff tell stories of past successes and the emphasis is on practical ideas and finding the best of what is currently happening.

**Proactive:** People are invited to imagine what the future might be like and how to redesign the organization to bring about these aspirations. With a positive atmosphere, staff can take risks and share every possible solution.

**Collaborative:** Everybody is involved from the senior management right down to the youngest and most junior member of staff.

The last aspect is probably one of the reasons why AI works so well. Although nobody likes change being imposed, if we are involved from the start, have our say, are listened to, and become part of the team that finds the solution, we will not only go along with any innovations but positively embrace them. The following diagram shows how AI works in practice:

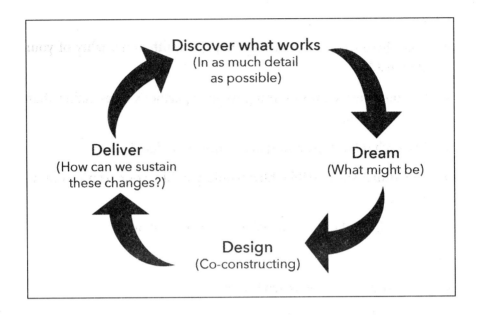

## AI and Your Relationship

This process works best when there is a long-running or difficult issue to resolve. Start by agreeing to put all negatives to one side for the next hour. (If anything negative does come up, write it down and discuss it on another occasion.) Next work your way around the AI circle:

**Discover what works**

🌹 Tell each other stories about the good times in your relationship.

🌹 Think of the peak experiences or the high points. In those experiences, discuss the things that you valued most about a) yourself and b) your partner.

🌹 Ask each other: What was good about those times? What else was good about it?

🌹 Think about the core factors that give "life" to your relationship and the other positive values on which to build.

**Dream**

🌱 What three wishes would heighten the health and vitality of your relationship?

🌱 Put your energy into listening to your partner's ideas rather than debating them.

🌱 Give each other time and space to dream in detail.

🌱 If anything was possible, how would you like your relationship to be?

🌱 What is important to you? Why do you care about it?

**Design**

🌱 What would help you reach this goal?

🌱 What skills can you each draw on?

🌱 How can you help each other?

🌱 What do you both agree on?

**Deliver**

🌱 What is the next step?

🌱 How could you reach that goal?

🌱 What problems might occur?

🌱 How could you overcome them?

🌱 How would you know that things have been resolved?

🌱 What do you need to talk about at a future occasion?

## AI in Action

Gemma and Paul had been together for three years but Paul has a child from a previous relationship. Unfortunately, his ex still had strong feelings for him and would frequently text—either messages of "undying love" or "goodbye forever." It was creating a lot of tension between Gemma and Paul. "I have to keep on friendly terms with my ex or she could make it very difficult for me to see my son," explained Paul. "Except I never know when he's going to get a text and whether his bad mood is a work problem, something I've done or another text from her," said Gemma. "It's like she can come into my house any time she wants." The ex-partner's destructive behavior had moved up a gear since Paul and Gemma had married. Although there were plenty of problems to explore, I decided to put those to one side and focus on Appreciative Inquiry.

So in "Discover what works" I asked about a time when Paul and Gemma had had a good discussion about his ex. "He'd been very down—a bit of food poisoning—and I asked him whether he was feeling better and he opened up about the latest text," said Gemma.

"She wanted me to go to the beach with her and our son because 'fathers should teach their children to swim.' It had really upset me." Instead of having their usual disagreement or fight, this time they'd ended up having a cuddle instead.

Next in "Dream," Gemma and Paul discussed how they would like things to be. "I don't want her to keep coming between us," said Paul, "so we can focus more on what's really important: you and me."

Gemma had a wish: "I'd like you to tell me more about the texts."

At this point, I had to intervene or they would have gone into their regular negative territory (where Paul complained that Gemma got wound up and angry over the texts and she would complain it was because she was continually excluded). Fortunately, they accepted that under AI their usual rows were banned. Gemma, instead, gave us another positive dream: "I'd like to get to know your son better and for the three of us to spend more time together."

With "Design," we looked at what had worked when they'd talked and then cuddled. "I was open and timely about the text," said Paul, "normally I would have stewed over it or told Gemma weeks later."

"I acknowledged how upsetting it is not to see much of his son or to be there to teach him to swim," said Gemma. "I also stopped to process the information before reacting." Instead of assuming that Paul wanted to go to the beach with his ex and his son—as she might have done when things were bad between her and Paul—Gemma had checked it out.

"It would be entirely inappropriate for me to go the beach with her, and anyway, the only person I want to be with is you," said Paul.

Finally in "Deliver," they discussed how to make their dream of better communication about Paul's ex come true. After explaining why he normally kept the texts to himself—"I don't want to break her confidences"—Paul decided to forward them onto Gemma for a trial period. Although she had asked for this outcome before, it emerged naturally out of the AI process because Paul had been involved in reaching this conclusion, rather than having had it imposed. Meanwhile, Gemma agreed to bring up only the most pressing texts and pledged her continuing support for Paul.

Another example of AI in action is Aidan and Miranda, both in their early forties, who came into counseling because they had drifted apart. Instead of looking at the problems in their relationship, I focused on what was working. They both had successful careers in New York and two children who were eleven and nine. "I really enjoy the time we spend together," said Miranda, "but we don't get to do it that often because we're both tired." I stopped her—as she was about to cross over into the negative—and encouraged her to tell me the story of a good time.

"I helped the children make pancakes in the kitchen and Aidan laid the table and ran to the corner store for honey. Our youngest had trouble tossing her pancake and Aidan helped and teased her that it would hit the ceiling," said Miranda.

"The children were finally exhausted and went up to bed early. Instead of clearing up, we opened a bottle of wine and put some music on and slow danced," added Aidan.

So I encouraged them to start to "Dream" about how life might be in ten years' time.

"I really want to have a future with you," said Aidan.

Miranda visibly relaxed. I asked her why?

"I sometimes thought he was there out of habit, convenience."

"It's good to hear it said out loud?" I asked.

She nodded.

In "Design," Aidan decided to work on his weight: "I really want to be around to enjoy a long future with Miranda and a healthy one too."

Suddenly, Miranda was able to get away from work more often and in "Deliver" they managed more weekends away in the countryside.

## EXERCISE APPRECIATIVE INQUIRY QUIZ

AI is built around thought-provoking questions that focus attention on what works and opens up discussion on how to build on success. This is why the wording has to be carefully thought through. Look at the following questions or prompts and decide which are the best framed.

1. In general, which is the best way to start a discussion about a topic?

   **a)** Yes/No option   **d)** Which?   **g)** When?

   **b)** How?   **e)** Who?   **h)** Why?

   **c)** What if?   **f)** What?   **i)** Where?

2. When talking about the future of your children, which best suits Appreciative Inquiry?

   **a)** Are our children getting the best education?

   **b)** Describe a time when our children were flourishing at school.

   **c)** What supports their learning?

   **d)** Why do they sometimes get poor grades?

   **d)** What would it be like if …?

## Answers

**Question One:**

"What if" is probably the best way of framing a question because it invites our partner to dream.

"How" and "What" are excellent for focusing your discussion. "When," "Who," "Where" are all good too.

Be careful about "Why" as it can either make your partner defensive (as it can be interpreted as blame) and if she or he doesn't have a definitive answer, the discussion is shut down before it starts. So try substituting "What are the contributing factors" in place of "Why."

The least successful frame will prompt a Yes/No answer and narrow rather than broaden the discussion.

**Question Two:**

Although all the questions could have prompted a discussion, some are better than others. I have listed them from most to least helpful:

a) This a great prompt because it fulfills the first part of the AI: Discover what works.

b) Another winner because it opens up the discussion.

c) This is an OK question because it is open. However, it can also be a sneaky way of introducing a favored outcome. (For example: "What would it be like if we got them some private tuition?") This could close down the conversation too quickly and not allow time for other, possibly better, options to emerge.

d) Unfortunately, "why" questions encourage faultfinding and blame. (For example, "The grades are poor because you don't help them enough with their homework" or "They mix with the wrong crowd.")

e) This is the least successful question as it prompts a Yes/No or Agree/Disagree answer.

## SUMMING UP

When we focus on what doesn't work, we not only take for granted what does, but treat it as normal and therefore don't truly understand the pleasures and resources of our relationship. Remembering the good times can help you dream and rediscover your desire for each other. In general, carrots (positives) provide a better incentive for change than sticks (negatives). However, be wary of offering too big a favor as nobody likes to be bribed.

## IN A NUTSHELL:

- Don't keep positive feedback to yourself.

- When something goes smoothly, go back over it in your mind's eye. What helped make it a success? How could you build on that for the future?

- We resist change when it is done to us rather than with us. So involve your partner in your dreams.

# CHAPTER TEN

## Change Your Behavior

When there is a problem in your relationship, it is easy to come up with a list of your partner's failings. When your attempts to resolve disputes hit a brick wall, it is tempting to think: "If only he would ..." or "everything would be better if she didn't ..." However, this keeps the focus on your partner: his or her stubbornness, unwillingness to open up, or some particularly annoying habit.

My next love hack is never popular when I introduce it at workshops or in counseling sessions, but that doesn't stop it from being very powerful: don't focus on his or her half of the equation, but look at your half instead. After all, as the old saying goes: "the only person you can change is yourself."

## ACHIEVING BALANCE

Most people arrive at my counseling office with complaints about their partner's behavior. A typical example is Julie, thirty-three, whose husband had cheated on her with a woman fifteen years older on seven or eight occasions during their six-year marriage: "I'm finding it difficult to understand his motive. When I ask the usual searching questions—'is she better in bed, more attractive?'—you would think I had asked him to drink a cup of cold sick. I am seriously querying my own judgment. I can't believe I've given birth to this man's child and he has the cheek to cheat on me! I have been tempted to get my revenge but not risen to it, but I have to say that all bets are off." After getting that off her chest, Julie took a deep breath and asked: "Why won't he open up to me?"

I asked her to describe her husband.

"He is the type of person who is terrible at showing his emotions," she said.

What about you?

"I'm fairly confrontational and particularly good at putting people on the spot. In fact, I've given him an ultimatum that before I decide whether I can continue with our relationship I need an explanation as to why he has never been faithful."

Faced with this threat, it was not surprising that her husband had trouble opening up. I asked Julie if there was any connection between her being "confrontational" and her husband being "terrible at showing emotions." She did a double take. Quite understandably, Julie had been concentrating on her husband's unacceptable behavior and did not realize how her communication style was making him clam up.

Another person unaware of the link between her behavior and her partner's was Bella. Her husband, Jeff, had announced that he was unhappy and to her immense frustration could not decide whether he wanted to try to save the marriage or to leave. Not surprisingly, she was confused: "One moment I'm up, one moment I'm down. If we're watching television, I wonder if I should be saying something but then I'm worrying about forever bringing up our problems and making him angry. In the meantime, there is an awkward silence. Should I say something? Should I stay quiet?" While Bella was turning herself inside out trying to fix the problems in her marriage what was her husband doing? "He just mopes about the house and occasionally moans: 'I've been a terrible husband. I've been a terrible father.' I try to reassure him but it does no good." In fact, Jeff was sinking deeper into depression. Although he had triggered the problem, Jeff had no need to put any thought or energy into solving it because Bella had taken all the responsibility for fixing things between them.

I ask people like Julie and Bella to imagine that they are on a seesaw. The more they push down on their side—pushing for an answer or trying to fix their relationship—the more their partner flies up on the other side. In Julie's partner's case, this was closing down and in Bella's, Jeff became even less interested in finding a solution.

So what's the answer? Instead of retreating into an exaggerated, almost cartoon version of yourself, head toward the middle of the seesaw as this will allow your partner to give up his or her extreme position too.

Julie was skeptical: "But if I don't push, I'll never get an answer." However, she agreed to be less confrontational and to see what happened. At the next week's session, she was all smiles: "I just listened, nodded my head, and kept quiet when he said something and somehow he opened up," she explained. Her husband had had occasional problems maintaining an erection. "He wanted to please me so much, this would make him anxious and he'd find it harder to perform. Because he didn't really care about the other woman, he didn't worry and had no problems—in some rather sick way, the sex with her made him feel more of a man."

Although Julie did not particularly like her husband's answer, it did help her move on and begin to address the problems underlying her husband's affair. (For more help on this topic read *How Can I Ever Trust You Again? Infidelity: From discovery to recovery in seven steps.*)

Meanwhile, Bella took a step back and instead of trying to solve Jeff's unhappiness, she began to accept her own dissatisfaction with the marriage. "We have both become very good at playing happy families," she explained. Once she was honest about her issues, Jeff realized it was not all "his fault" and decided to come into counseling. Instead of fixing the marriage being Bella's project, it became a joint one. They were no longer at opposite ends of a seesaw; they had achieved balance.

## EXERCISE GETTING OFF THE SEESAW

Once you and your partner are polarized on opposite ends of a seesaw, it becomes harder and harder to change. This exercise will help break this unhelpful pattern:

1. **Recognize your seesaw.** Some of the common ones include: Bringing Up Problems/Containing Problems; Spender/Saver; Independence/Togetherness (one partner stresses the importance of "me" time and the other "us" time); Optimist/Pessimist. This is just a small selection. What is your seesaw?

2. **Accept the equal importance of your partner's position.** If a couple never brought up problems, nothing would get solved. However, if they argued about everything—and there was no sense of proportion—life would be equally impossible. Similarly, if a couple did nothing but spend, they would become bankrupt. However, if they were both keen on saving—and were unable to enjoy their money—life would be equally miserable. What are the advantages of your partner's position?

3. **Experiment.** Instead of retreating to your end of the seesaw and worrying, for example, that relaxing your grip on the budget strings will make your partner go crazy, discover what happens if you listen to your partner, hear her or his fears, and find a joint solution.

4. **Become a little bit more like your partner.** This will allow her or him to change and become a little bit more like you.

## TALKING AT CROSS-PURPOSES

If you're frustrated about your partner's actions but uncertain how your behavior might be contributing, Transactional Analysis, or TA for short, can be a real eye-opener. In the 1950s, an American psychiatrist called Eric Berne proposed that all our thoughts, feelings, and behavior come from three distinct parts of our personality: "Parent," "Adult," and "Child." (The idea is similar to Freud's super ego, ego, and id.)

Christmas, for example, is one of the few times when all three parts of our personality come equally to the fore. We indulge our inner child with presents and allow its creativity free reign with decorations and party games. At the same time, our inner parent has a lot to organize and almost naturally slips into two types of behavior. Berne calls these: Nurturing Parent (Don't worry, I'll buy a present for your mom) and Critical Parent (You've laid the table all wrong). Finally, we need the adult part of our personality, which is objective and rational, to help us navigate through all the alcohol, rich food, and heightened emotions. Berne stresses the importance of all three parts of our personality and, indeed, keeping the "Parent," "Adult," and "Child" in harmony makes for a well-rounded individual. The problem is how we use them to communicate with other people.

If you and your partner are both using the same parts of your personality, everything is fine. For example, at a boring party, your inner child meets the eye of your partner's inner child and both decide to put some music on and get everybody dancing. Berne calls this a *Concordant Transaction.*

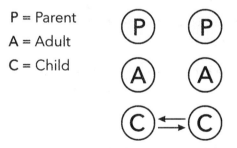

P = Parent
A = Adult
C = Child

A variation on this relatively straightforward type of communication is when one partner's inner child complains: "I'll never get all these done" and the other's nurturing parent will reply: "Never mind,

I'll sort it out." This is called a *Parallel Transaction* and, in theory, this kind of communication could continue happily for years.

P = Parent
A = Adult
C = Child

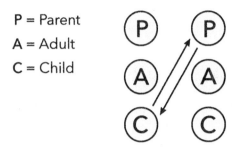

The problems come from what Berne calls *Crossed Transactions.* For example, the "Adult" part of your personality asks: "Have you seen my keys?" However, instead of replying with his or her inner adult, your partner responds: "You shouldn't leave things lying about"—which is "critical parent"—or "Why do you blame me for everything?" which is "inner child."

P = Parent
A = Adult
C = Child

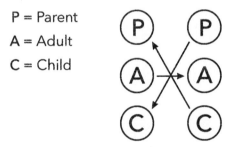

At this point, we need to look in more detail about the three parts of our personality. In the same way that there are two types of parent (Nurturing and Critical) there are also two types of child. Berne calls these the Free Child (the source of creativity, joy, and fun) and the Adapted Child (which has learned to sulk, moan, and manipulate). However, there is only one adult mode —which is rational and good at making decisions.

## How to Spot Which Part of Your Personality Is In Play

It is not just the words that betray which part of our personality is at the fore, but also the tone of our voice, facial expressions, and general body language:

| | PARENT | | ADULT | CHILD | |
|---|---|---|---|---|---|
| | *Critical Parent* | *Nurturing Parent* | | *Free Child* | *Adapted Child* |
| **Words** | Should, don't, you can't, if I were you | Let me help you, don't worry, there-there | How, when, why, what are the facts, options | Wow, brilliant, you'll never guess | Sorry, if only, it's not my fault |
| **Tones of Voice** | Stern, harsh, judgmental, indignant | Soothing, soft, caring, sympathetic | Clear, inquiring, assertive | Laughter, energetic, excited | Appealing, placating, protesting |
| **Body Language** | Finger pointing, hands on hips, rolling eyes upward | Open arms, nodding, touching | Level eye contact, confident appearance, active listening | Bright eyed, exaggerated motions, spontaneous | Downcast eyes, pouting, slumped shoulders |

# TA IN ACTION

Once you can read which part of the personality is speaking and which responding, how can you use this knowledge to improve your relationships? Luke and Allen are a gay couple in their mid-thirties who have been together for five years. Luke is very family orientated and likes to go round to his parents for Sunday dinner but Allen feels that Luke's parents do not really accept their relationship.

"Why do I want to spend time with people who barely tolerate me?" complained Allen.

"They're doing their best," replied Luke.

"So why after all these years do you still need to tell them to buy me a birthday present?" Alan said and then turned to me, "But what I really hate is the way that he regresses to being ten years old again when he's with his parents."

Luke's parents were certainly in critical parent mode; meanwhile Luke himself was slipping into one of the two types of inner child responses.

When I explained TA to this couple, they immediately spotted than Luke was in adapted child mode.

"See, it's what have I've been telling you," Allen said, "and this has got to stop."

"Which part of your personality is talking?" I asked.

Allen suddenly laughed as he recognized that this outburst came straight from his own critical parent.

Instead of having the same old argument, they both accessed their adult mode and decided is was better to invite Luke's parents to their house. At the next counseling session, we used TA to examine what happened.

"My mother was a little snide about the mashed potatoes," explained Luke. "Rather than ignoring her or taking out my bad mood on Allen, I asked my mother: 'Is there a problem?'" In effect, he had accessed the adult part of his personality. Interestingly, by not responding as a child, he encouraged his mother to move into adult mode too. They had a long chat later while clearing up, and she admitted that she felt uncomfortable that her son cooked, as she saw this as "feminine."

Another example of TA helping a couple is Austin and Lorna. They are in their mid-forties and have a son who wanted to join the army. Austin believed they should support their son's choice and Lorna wanted to do everything to protect him.

"You've always been overprotective and smothered him," Austin complained.

"Is it any wonder, with the way that you're always on at him: push, push, push," Lorna came straight back. "Nothing is ever good enough for you. Have you ever asked why he wants to get away from us?"

With TA, they recognized their two styles of parenting: nurturing (not always positive as it can prevent children taking responsibility for themselves) and critical (not always negative as it can push children to grow and achieve). Just as important, we looked at the type of parenting that Luke and Lorna had received and how these experiences had fed into their behavior today.

In fact, another way of looking at the three parts of our personality is that "Parent" is life as we were taught, "Child" is life as we feel it, and "Adult" is life as we work it out for ourselves.

Although there many different TA combinations, there are two crossed transactions that are particularly common in my counseling room:

### My Partner Is Behaving Like a Sulky Teenager

"I already have two children, I don't need a third," Gabriella complained about her husband, Charlie. "When he comes home in the evening, I'm exhausted but he seldom volunteers to help—not even with the fun stuff like bathtime. And if I ask him a question—such as 'is the water too hot?'—he either explodes or sulks."

**Diagnosis:** If your partner behaves like a child, it might be that you're treating him or her like one.

**Solution:** Come out of parent mode (probably critical parent) and talk adult to adult.

### My Partner Is Always Talking Down to Me

"I asked my husband for help with my tax return and I got a lecture about keeping my paper work straight," said Piper. "It went from bad to worse and he started complaining about my 'attitude' but I just asked a simple question."

**Diagnosis:** If your partner treats you like a child, it could be that you've been acting like one.

**Solution:** Shift into talking adult to adult.

## How to Communicate Adult to Adult

Being in adult mode means asking directly and openly for something (wheedling, manipulating, and demanding are all childish behaviors). It means accepting our partner is equally capable and has similar or complementary skills (and therefore has a viewpoint that should be heard and respected). Adult behavior is also rational, inquiring, and open to negotiation.

For example, when Gabriella examined her own behavior—rather than focusing on Charlie's—she realized that she'd been supervising him rather than asking for his help. When she relaxed and let him get on with bathing the children his way, her husband volunteered more often to take over. Meanwhile, Gabriella could slowly switch over from being a mother into being one half of a couple. When bathtime was over, they would cuddle on the couch or share a bottle of wine.

When Piper looked at her behavior, she decided to get her paperwork straight and read the tax form before asking for help. In that way, she would have specific questions to ask her husband and have an adult-to-adult conversation.

## EXERCISE  TA QUIZ

Being able to spot the different parts of our personality—critical parent, nurturing parent, adult, free child, or adapted child—is the most important ingredient in changing our behavior. So look at the following scenarios and decide which part of the personality is in play:

**1.** When Angela's friend was stood up her boyfriend for the second time that month, Angela said: "I told you he was trouble."

**2.** When Edwin's wife's best friend dropped in in a terrible state— her long-term boyfriend had left their shared house and moved in with another woman—he recommended a lawyer who could advise on her rights.

**3.** Preston didn't want to renovate the kitchen; he thought the current one was fine and anyway they couldn't afford a new one. However, his wife put so much pressure on that he agreed to make a start. Except, he could never find the right weekend to start. There was always more pressing jobs and even the arrival of a new stove did nothing to speed him along.

**4.** When Patricia's brother-in-law died, she collected her sister from the hospice, took her home, and fed her and then drove from place to place to make all the arrangements for the funeral.

**5.** When there was a power outage during an important dinner party and Clara couldn't melt the chocolate for her profiteroles, she put a pot over her open fire. Later she encouraged everybody to tell ghost stories.

**ANSWERS:**
**These are the parts of the personality in play in scenarios above.**

1. Critical parent; 2. Adult; 3. Adapted child; 4. Nurturing parent; 5. Free child

It is worth pointing out that in the quiz, Angela, Edwin, Patricia, and Clara responded with the most appropriate mode of behavior for their circumstances. There are times when we need someone tell us we've made a mistake (critical parent) or to take over (nurturing parent). Free child is often fun and creative. Adult is rational and helps us take a considered look at a problem. Adapted child is more problematic. It can make us question authority and rebel against injustice but, in the example, Preston's procrastination just prolonged his problems rather than resolved them.

Ultimately, we need every one of these ways of responding in our tool kit. Problems arise when someone gets stuck in one mode.

# PEOPLE ARE OK

How we talk to our partner has a big impact on how our partner reacts. If we treat him or her well, he or she will return the favor. However, self-interest alone should not drive our behavior—rather a fundamental belief that our partner deserves our respect. This is a second important idea embedded in Transactional Analysis: **"People are OK."** By this, Berne means that everybody has worth, value, and dignity. At first sight, this is not such a radical idea. However, while we're happy to sign up for "worth, value, and dignity" for all mankind, we're not necessarily so compassionate toward ourselves and our family. So while "People are OK" at a universal level should translate down to the personal and relationship level as **"I'm OK, You're OK"** (the title of a famous book written by Thomas A. Harris, a long-term friend and associate of Berne), it often becomes:

I'm not OK, You're not OK

I'm not OK, You're OK

I'm OK, You're not OK

## The Impact of Believing "I'm Not OK"

When deep down someone believes that they are "not OK," there are normally two ways of coping. The first is to accept the label—which has been pinned on by parents, teachers, and lovers—and become depressed. The second is to fight back and expend a lot of energy trying to prove to yourself and the world at large that you are "OK" after all. Unfortunately, the internal picture of being "not OK" is so strong that anything beyond top of the class, most-talented newcomer, employee of the month, or mom of the year equals complete failure. The only option is to strive harder and harder and become a perfectionist.

If it is tough being a perfectionist, it is even tougher being the partner of one. "My husband hates mess so much that I make certain that the kids tidy up all of their toys half and hour before Vincent gets home," says Mica. "I'm reasonably tidy, I like to keep things straight, but he is fanatical." Normally the partners of perfectionists are fairly laid-back—as it would be impossible for two perfectionists to live together—and do their best to accommodate their partner's whims. However, the obsessive behavior can grind them down. "Even Vincent's friends have a go at him—especially after he insisted on going home from the bar and getting changed after he got a bit of beer over his shirt," says Mica.

If you're a perfectionist, ask yourself: Am I concentrating on my partner's behavior to avoid looking at myself? When Vincent became more aware of his own behavior and stopped trying to control Mica and his children, he couldn't help but focus on the high standards he set himself and how often he felt a failure. "When I was a kid, my mother spent a lot of time making me look adorable. Little buttoned-up coat. Polished shoes. She was always wiping my face with the corner of her handkerchief," says Vincent. "She would be so proud of me but she'd explode if I so much as stepped in a puddle or my school cap wasn't straight."

"Did it seem that she only loved you when you were neat and tidy?" I asked.

Vincent didn't reply; he started crying.

Time and again, it seems that being a perfectionist is like carpeting the whole world to avoid getting a thorn in your foot—rather than putting on a pair of shoes. In other words, rather than trying to bend everybody else to your standards, put that energy into understanding yourself, giving yourself a little more leeway, and developing a thicker skin so that when things don't or can't go your way, rejection does not feel so personal. There is more about improving self-esteem in another book in this series: *Learn to Love Yourself Enough*.

## The Impact of Believing "You're Not OK"

If you believe your partner is not OK, you are going to want to change him or her. After all, you have plenty of evidence of bad or unsavory behavior and it is quite reasonable to want to make changes ... or is it? Before you get angry and throw this book across the room, let me explain. If people have worth, value, and dignity then your partner must have those qualities too—but somehow you have become blinded to them.

So what's happening? Our common-sense understanding of the world sees a simple link between an event and how it makes us feel. For example, Gemma, from the previous chapter, would get upset every time Paul received a text from his ex.

$$\text{Event} \longrightarrow \text{Emotion}$$

$$\text{Text} \longrightarrow \text{Upset}$$

However, in reality, the picture is more complicated. There is no direct relationship between an event and emotion. Everything is filtered through our own particular interpretation. For example, Gemma thought that Paul was too friendly to his ex and that encouraged her to hope for a reconciliation. She worried that his ex would "forever" be interfering in their marriage and this would "spoil" everything.

$$\text{Event} \longrightarrow \text{Interpretation} \longrightarrow \text{Emotion}$$

$$\text{Text} \longrightarrow \text{Ruin our marriage} \longrightarrow \text{Upset}$$

When Gemma could accept that Paul was OK and there might be some merit in remaining on friendly terms—rather than fighting through the courts for access to his son—she found the texts less upsetting. With the temperature in the house lowered, Paul found it easier to talk to Gemma. She could acknowledge his position and he could listen to hers. Instead of being on opposite sides, they became a team. "In fact, these problems have brought us closer together," Gemma smiled. By changing her interpretation, she had transformed her reaction:

$$\text{Text} \longrightarrow \text{Opportunity to bond} \longrightarrow \text{Sympathy for Paul}$$

## Challenge Your Opinion of Your Partner

If deep down you think your partner is "not OK" ask yourself: What is the evidence? To help challenge your interpretation put your "evidence" to this test:

1. What is going through my mind and how much do I believe it?

2. What supports this view?

3. What contradicts my conclusions?

4. How might someone else interpret this situation?

5. What evidence is there to support alternatives?

6. What would I advise someone else to do?

7. What evidence is there to support alternative views?

8. How does my thinking help or hinder achieving my goals?

9. What effect would believing an alternative have?

10. What can I do differently?


## EXERCISE   RESPONSIBILITY PIE

For a fresh look at a particularly thorny problem between you and your partner, imagine a pie, which has been divided into slices to reflect how much or how little "responsibility" should be apportioned to each of the following:

| | |
|---|---|
| My Partner | Other People |
| Myself | Circumstances |
| Family | Greater Culture |

This is what happened when Gemma did this exercise about the text messages:

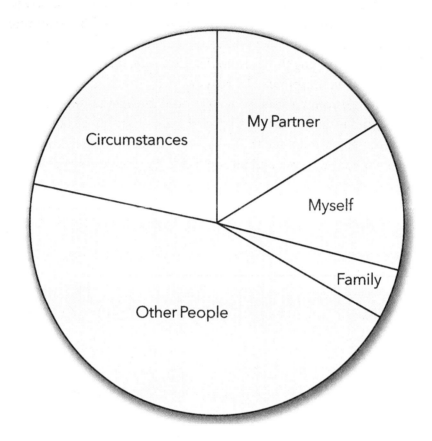

However you slice up your pie, it is always more complicated than just blaming your partner or indeed yourself.

## SUMMING UP

Under stress, we can become a more exaggerated version of ourselves. Unfortunately, this encourages our partners to respond by becoming more extreme too. Although we imagine that holding on to our view is the only thing stopping things from deteriorating, it is also preventing the situation from improving. By moving to a more balanced position, this will free up your partner to change too. Time and again, changing your interpretation of your partner's behavior—from something negative to something more neutral—will change your reaction, lower the temperature in the house, and make it easier to resolve the problem.

## IN A NUTSHELL:

- When communication is going wrong, switch into "Adult" mode as this will encourage your partner to do the same.

- Instead of assuming the worse, check it out. Ask your partner what he or she means rather than jumping to conclusions.

- Sometimes if you change your attitude to your partner's behavior, it is less of a problem.

# CHAPTER ELEVEN

---

# Saving the Situation

In most circumstances, it is not so important what you are arguing about, but how. Keeping calm, listening to each other, and being assertive will triumph over most problems. However, there are some situations that merit special discussion and need specifically targeted love hacks.

## MONEY ISSUES

Financial problems are always difficult to discuss, partly because money worries permeate ever corner of a couple's life, but mainly because arguments are always about more than costs, spending priorities, and overdrafts.

Louise and Will, both in their mid-thirties, got into trouble when Louise's gave up working full-time after she had a baby. "We used to have plenty of money, foreign vacations, and plenty of time together," explains Louise, "but now we hardly see each other and when we do, we end up rowing about money. Yet the worst part is that I feel so helpless."

While Louise became a worrier, Will tried to cope with the crisis by switching off. "I'm under a lot of pressure at work, so I need to relax at home or my head will explode," he explains, "I'll play games on the computer or go off fishing at the weekend. OK, we've money problems, but what's the point of obsessing?"

Like most couples with financial problems, they are on a money seesaw. So that the more one partner pushes down on their end, the higher up (and more extreme) the other goes. In the case of Louise and Will, the more "unconcerned"—at least on the surface—that he became, the more "worried" she became. It had got to the point where they found it impossible to discuss their finances as even the slightest disagreement could turn nasty.

Nowhere is the money seesaw more marked than when couples becomes "Saver" and "Spender." Travis and Reese had been married for almost twenty years but had never really sorted their finances out. Travis believed that Reese's spending was out of control. "She's always coming back from the stores with piles of bags," he complained. "It's not like they're all for me," she countered. "I used to buy him something nice, such as a sweater, but he'd get so upset that I stopped." Unfortunately, whenever Travis got angry—normally after discovering Reese had taken out another loan—she got depressed and felt the need to raise her mood with another shopping trip. Their problems were made worse because they had no joint bank account and instead shuffled money between personal bank and savings accounts.

Another common seesaw is "wise" and "innocent" about money. On the surface, Juan, fifty-two, and Samantha, thirty-nine, should have had similar attitudes to money. They both had childhoods where finances were tight. Juan was the eldest of eight children and his mother struggled on his father's mail carrier's salary. Samantha's father owned a hairdressing salon but was an addict and gambled away all the profits. So her family had started in a detached house with a garden and ended up in public housing. However, they drew very different conclusions from their experiences. Juan became money "wise": reading the financial section of the newspaper, making investments, and putting money into a pension fund. Samantha became "innocent." "I know nothing about money," she joked. "If an item is reduced by twenty dollars that means I can spend the 'saved' money on something else." The more reckless that Samantha became, the more Juan felt the need to hoard money. "Sometimes I feel like a little girl, asking Daddy for an allowance," Samantha complained.

## How to Defuse Arguments About Money

The first step is to understand that money means different things to different people. I ask couples to tell each other a story from their childhood. Juan remembered getting a paper route and the extra food it bought. So I asked him what money meant. "Power," he answered. Samantha told about the pleasure from a shiny new bicycle for her tenth birthday and the pain of discovering three weeks later that her father had sold it. So what did money mean to her? "Enjoy it while you can," she concluded. Other meanings for money include: freedom, security, fun, a terrible responsibility, a way of keeping score, corrupting, status, respect. There are as many answers as there are people.

The next step is to identify your particular seesaw—worried/unconcerned, saver/spender, wise/innocent, hoarder/gambler—and your greatest fear about what would happen if your partner got his or her way. For Reese, the shopper, it was: "Everything will be gray and dour and with no joy." Her husband, Travis, was quick to reassure: "I don't want to stop all your spending." Travis's greatest fear was that the house would be repossessed. It was Reese's turn to calm him down: "I'm aware that my closet has got out of hand and I've started selling some excess clothes on eBay." Ultimately, they were able to see that both ends of the seesaw had value: without Travis' saving, they would be in serious financial hardship; without Reese's ability to enjoy money, there would be no treats and their lives would be very dull.

Another way of understanding your partner's position on the money seesaw is to examine her or his past. Although our take on money might seem fixed, it will often change from relationship to relationship—depending on the other person's personality and attitude to money. When Will, the man who escaped his money worries by fishing and computer games, looked back at his first marriage, he had a valuable insight. "She was entirely reckless and I had to keep a very firm hand," he remembered. In effect, he had been the "Worrier" in that relationship. He turned to Louise: "I'm sorry, it must be horrible for you. We should be doing this together." Ultimately, they had found a middle position where their seesaw could be balanced.

It is only at this point that the traditional solution for money worries—getting out the bills, bank statements, and calculator—can come into play. For the first time, Will explained the complexities of his company's sales commissions and why his salary changed each month. Louise felt less in the dark and more reassured. Meanwhile, Reese, the shopper, was able to reveal the extent of her debts to Travis—which turned out to be less than he feared. "Why didn't you tell me before?" asked Travis. "I would have felt judged," explained Reese. When they went through the monthly outgoings in their separate accounts, Travis accepted that the amount he contributed to their joint living expenses was inadequate. (Her debts were partially caused by funding items like their children's birthday presents out of the grocery allowance.) They also realized that their accounting system was a hangover from when they first came together and did not reflect the realities of family life. So they opened a joint account.

Ultimately, there is no right or wrong approach to finances. However, dealings need to be transparent and honest and this is only possible if both partners feel that their opinions have been heard and valued first.

## EXERCISE   ARE YOU FINANCIALLY COMPATIBLE?

Look at the following questions and write down your immediate thoughts on a separate piece of paper. Don't spend too long—your first response is the most revealing. Then give the quiz to your partner to complete and compare results. Discuss the differences and similarities in your attitudes to money, how you could meet in the middle, and whether you need to arrange your finances differently.

1. For me, money represents ... (write down your top three answers).

2. Look at the following lists and choose your top five spending

priorities: car, clothes, home improvements, socializing, eating out, sports/gym membership, saving/investing, gadgets, vacations, treats, items for the house, children.

3. How much does your partner bring home, after deductions, every month?

4. How much money is it acceptable to spend on items purely for yourself in an average month?

5. What is the largest amount you would spend on yourself without consulting your partner?

6. Without prior discussion, what is the most you would spend on something for the house or the children?

7. For me, debts are … (write down your feelings/attitude toward debt).

8. How much debt, excluding mortgage payments, do you think that you are carrying as a couple?

9. How much personal debt do you think your partner is carrying?

10. What is your greatest weakness concerning money?

## DEALING WITH IDENTITY ISSUES

This topic can come up as wanting more independence (because one partner feels smothered or controlled) or someone wondering: "Who am I" and "What do I want out of life?" In many cases, one or both partners are moving from one life stage to another. For example, becoming parents, turning forty, children leaving home, or a parent's death. All of these events naturally make someone take stock and look for something different. Unfortunately, it is easy for this introspection to turn into simmering resentment, emotional exhaustion, and a relationship crisis.

If it is your partner who seems, almost overnight, to have turned into a stranger it can be very unsettling. So how should you respond? Ask yourself: Does my partner have a valid point or a reasonable request? Try to separate legitimate desires—such as retraining, bettering oneself, or trying something new—from what might seem like a personal attack on you.

For example, Owen felt threatened because his wife, Khloe, wanted to return to college once their two children were old enough to attend school. He put up lots of practical reasons for her staying at home: costs, what if one of the children got sick, and how studying would eat into their couple time. Their arguments soon became about Owen being controlling or holding Khloe back, rather than the original issue of returning to college. Behind the anger about a partner changing, there is almost always fear. So ask yourself: What am I afraid of? Telling your partner about these fears will probably provide reassurance—rather than another round of arguments—and the platform to discuss the changes properly.

## How to Defuse Identity Issues

What if it is you who wants to change? Grand gestures, like moving abroad or ending a relationship, often just take the compliant or controlling behavior to another country or another relationship. Identity is accumulated through small victory after small victory: standing up for yourself, doing something different from what other people expect, understanding your fears and your partner's fears. Here are some pointers on the way:

- ☙ **Look at your internal dialogue:** Do you spend more time second-guessing your partner's reaction than examining your own feelings? Do you find yourself trying to "hold the line," frightened that if you give in over one thing that it will have a domino effect and change everything.

- ☙ **Identify which of the unhelpful argument patterns that you and your partner fall into:** Understanding a behavior is halfway to changing it. Even if next time you find yourself falling into the old patterns, keep one eye on observing yourself. This will make you doubly aware of the pitfalls and less likely to fall into the same traps next time around.

- 🌱 **Take responsibility:** Don't cast yourself as the victim, look at your contribution to the pattern. As the old saying goes: you can't change anybody but yourself.

- 🌱 **Try to understand, instead of trying to convince/cajole/control each other:** Without understanding, it is impossible to build a proper compromise. (For more on this see "Break Out of Controlling Behavior" in the next exercise.)

- 🌱 **Look at the expectations that underpin your view of the world and yourself:** Where does each expectation come from? How much of your identity has come from your parents? How much from your friends? How much from our wider culture, religion, the media? How much of this belongs to you?

- 🌱 **Aim for a compromise:** Is there a middle way that would balance individual and couple identity?

This process helped Stacey and Carl find a way through Stacey's identity crisis. They had been together since they were eighteen, but at twenty-five, Stacey felt they were like an old married couple. Her internal dialogue was full of questions such as: "Is it OK to want to go out this often?" "Will Carl be upset with me for wanting to go?" Carl's internal dialogue had gone along similar lines: "Should I say something about her going out so much?" and "What will she think about me if I ask her to stay in?" From the beginning of their relationship, Carl and Stacey had both been so keen to please each other that their relationship had been Compliance/Compliance. More recently, Stacey had run up large credit card bills and Carl had tried to keep spending down: Rebellion/Control.

Next, with "Taking Responsibility," Stacey admitted that her shopping had been like that of a reckless teenager, and Carl, that he had been a critical parent; this allowed them to have an adult-to-adult discussion that created a proper budget and put aside money for entertainment. During "Understanding," Carl learned that nights in front of the TV made Stacey feel old before her time; Stacey learned that Carl thought they should be saving to start a family. We had finally reached the unspoken expectations that had been driving them apart. Where had these expectations come from? Carl's parents had had children in their mid-twenties and, as he said, "It just feels the right time." However, Stacey's mother had regretted having children early and had always advised her daughter to "see something of the world first."

Finally, the couple were ready for a compromise. Carl started joining Stacey for some of her nights out and saving for a trip to the UK. Stacey agreed that she would like to have children before she turned thirty.

Meanwhile, Khloe and Owen, who argued about her plans to return to college, just needed a frank discussion about both of their fears. Khloe was able to reassure Owen that she was not planning to leave and he was able to be more supportive. Khloe decided to start carving her own individual identity by taking an extra high school diploma part time at local evening classes. "I wanted to check motherhood had not completely destroyed all my brain cells," she explained, "but also to check I really want this before we splash out a lot of money." Owen was happy to babysit on her college nights.

## BREAK OUT OF CONTROLLING BEHAVIOR

The object of this exercise is to understand both your partner's behavior and your own. Take an issue that causes a lot of tension between the two of you—something that you have argued about frequently in the past or need to argue about!

- The partner who is having an identity crisis or wanting change starts. If this is both of you, flip a coin. He or she talks about how they see the problem, what they want and how they feel. The other person just listens.

- The listener can ask for amplification or clarification but nothing else. No defending, no answering back, no comforting or reassuring. Just listening and understanding.

- If the person who is listening feels tempted to speak, he or she should first ask themselves: Am I trying to convince or defend? If the answer is yes, bite your tongue. If the question aims to clarify or to dig deeper, feel free to speak.

- When there is a lull in the conversation, check that you have properly understood your partner. "What you are saying is ..." "Have I understood properly that you feel ...?"

- If an argument starts, stop and look at the protecting patterns (outlined in Chapter One): Control/Compliance; Control/Control; Indifference/Indifference; Control/Rebellion. Have you fallen into one of these traps?

- The object of the exercise is not to find a solution to the difference but to understand.

- On many occasions the problems disappear without any action plan. This is because understanding the reasons behind our partner's contentious behavior makes it easier to tolerate. Often our tolerance makes our partner soften their behavior, which in turn increases our tolerance and sets up a virtuous circle.

If you are working through this book alone, put yourself in the listening position. Ask your partner why he or she feels so strongly about a point of dispute and follow the exercise from there. If your partner refuses: "You know only too well," explain that you want to double-check that you understand—this will take them off the defensive. When you've finished hearing and truly understand all their viewpoints ask: "Could I explain where I am coming from?" If your partner feels understood, he or she will be open to offering the same courtesy to you. So if your partner refuses to listen, keep trying to understand before seeking to be understood.

# IRRECONCILABLE DIFFERENCES

This book focuses on resolving relationship problems by teaching communication techniques and helping you to look through your partner's eyes, but what if there is an important area where your views are diametrically opposed and where there seems to be no middle way. Does this mean that your relationship is ultimately doomed? It is easy to be downhearted, but there are still lots of grounds for hope.

Amy and Harry, in their mid-thirties, had a basically good relationship. They loved each other and their two children but one stumbling block threatened their whole relationship: sailing. "There is nothing that I enjoy more than being at sea," explained Harry. "I can forget about all my problems at work and just be myself." Unfortunately, Amy was not a natural born sailor and didn't want her weekends dominated by a boat: "The girls aren't that keen either." Harry quickly countered: "But they haven't been on a proper trip—just up and down the river." Even the most unlikely dispute would turn into another chance to debate the pros and cons of sailing. So I decided to ban the topic. "Shouldn't we sort out this first as it's causing us all this trouble," said Harry. "If we can't, I don't think there is any future for us," added Amy. (This is the sort of hopeless talk that I was seeking to avoid.)

After much discussion, they agreed to concentrate on the other issues between them. I had expected to spend only a couple of weeks improving their argument skills, but I was surprised at how many other differences had been masked by the boat. For example, Harry thought that Amy was too soft on the children and she thought he was too quick to discipline. Other contentious areas included how to spend evenings and their respective in-laws. Previously these differences had fed into their arguments about sailing ("Don't talk to the kids like that, you're not captain of the ship") and the resulting row would quickly become insoluble. With the ban in place, they were able to listen to each other better and make concessions without Harry fearing he'd never be allowed to sail again and Amy worrying about only seeing him if she put up with a cold and wet boat. After a couple of months, they not only became better at resolving everyday disputes but the general tension reduced significantly. They were ready to tackle their irreconcilable difference.

Instead of allowing Harry and Amy to replay their old arguments—we knew where that would lead—we broke the pattern by doing a brainstorm. I stood by the flip chart and asked for solutions. Harry suggested buying a half share with his father in a marina closer to home and thereby cutting down traveling time. Amy wanted to dispute those calculations. However, the rules of a brainstorm prevent immediate evaluation. Every idea, however impractical or off-the-wall, is written up. Amy suggested waiting until the children were older before buying a boat. Harry wanted to object but I reminded him of the rules and wrote it up. It is important to value every suggestion because it can trigger something better—which it did for Harry and Amy. Harry thought the children were old enough to crew a boat—as long as it was somewhere calm. Amy suggested Florida: "At least it will be warm, and who knows, they might like it."

Finally, they were able to reach a compromise and agree to a two-part summer vacation with one week hiring a boat and one week on dry land at a resort hotel. Like many couples, when we finally came to the irreconcilable problem, as long as communication had been improved, all the problems melted away. In fact, for Harry and Amy, the final discussions were almost an anticlimax.

## FALLING OUT OF LOVE

Often in an attempt to gain control of an out of control situation, the person trying to save a relationship will magnify their weaknesses and promise to change overnight. When Tony told Maria that he had fallen out of love with her, he also confessed that he was unhappy with their sex life. She jumped on this scrap of information, read a million books, and promised a better future. Maria was truly in overdrive, overwhelming Tony with love, and hoping to win him back. For fear of embarrassing Tony in front of their friends, Maria also kept her problems to herself. Although thoughtful, this decision proved to be counterproductive. Her friends would have stopped her from taking all the blame and humiliating herself into the bargain. Remember the first of my three laws of relationship disputes (see Chapter One): all arguments are "six of one and half a dozen of the other." Tony needed to take blame for not speaking up sooner and some responsibility for their inadequate sex life.

So how do you deal with a partner who is so profoundly unhappy that he is she is considering leaving? Start thinking about the changes that you would like. This surprises many clients who would rather keep the spotlight on their partners. Maria was particularly reluctant to talk about her issues: "If I tell him my problems, he'll think the situation is hopeless. No. I've got to concentrate on the positive." But this can easily be seen as dismissing the crisis or even worse—not really listening. After some prompting, Maria began to think about her needs too. "Tony keeps himself to himself, I don't know what he's thinking of half the time," she explained. "When he doesn't share his feelings with me, I don't really feel like sharing my body with him." Finally, both Maria and Tony had something concrete to improve and their relationship began to turn around. Tony would chat about his day on his return from work, while Maria would try one of the tips from her magazine, for example: keeping good eye contact during their lovemaking (rather than closing them or turning her head away). The following week, Maria and Tony came back with smiles on their faces. He had talked and she had looked and both felt more intimate than they had for years.

The plan had worked because it had fulfilled three basic requirements:

## 1. The needs had been expressed as a positive

When you tell your partner, for example, "you don't talk to me," it doesn't matter how nicely you put it—he or she will hear this as a criticism. The natural response to criticism is either to get defensive or to attack back. However, a positive request, such as "I'd really like to understand more about your job," invites a positive response.

## 2. They had asked for something concrete

Some requests, even though they are positive, fail because the other partner has no real idea where to start. For example: "I'd like us to spend more time together" is fine, but how long, how often, and what will the couple do? Contrast this with: "I'd like us to walk the dog together on Saturday morning."

## 3. It had been small and easy to do

Instead of offering something ambitious, like a new position for intercourse or sexy lingerie, Maria had agreed to something she knew would be achievable: keeping her eyes open. Instead of intimate chats about love and where the relationship was going, Tony had agreed to talk about something more neutral: his work.

Whether you are coming back from a crisis or defusing a minor spat, the following exercise is very useful.

## THE POWER OF ACKNOWLEDGING

Over thirty years of couple counseling has shown me that there is nothing more powerful in turning around a difficult situation than the power of acknowledging. It not only shows that you are open-hearted, but helps open up the heart of the other person too. Best of all, it can shift a relationship out of crisis mode and into a phase where both parties can truly listen to each other. So how does it work?

Lizzie, forty-two, has been dating Thomas, forty-five, for twelve months and they came into counseling because they could not decide whether to live together. Their relationship was complicated because both had children from previous marriages and Lizzie had a twelve-year-old autistic child. "He has a mental age of about three or four which means that he is hard work and I can't give Thomas the attention that he seems to demand. I don't think he understands just how exhausting it is for me, day in, day out. There is no letup." Thomas kept his eyes fixed on the floor and muttered: "I do know what it's like." For a while, each partner kept on repeating their basic case—with more and more supporting evidence. Eventually, I threw up my hands: "What did they want from each other?"

"I just want Lizzie to understand how hard I've tried," said Thomas. With a little prompting, Lizzie did acknowledge that Thomas was patient, kind, and supportive and went on to list examples and occasions when she'd been particularly grateful. Thomas, in turn, acknowledged, how much Lizzie had achieved with her son. Obviously, both had known deep down that the other appreciated them, but they needed to hear it! Finally, Lizzie and Thomas were ready to negotiate with open hearts and soon found a formula for living together. Here are the ingredients for acknowledging:

- **It has to be neutral.** Rather than said angrily, sarcastically, or with strings attached.

- **It works best with examples.** Instead of just thank you for being helpful—which is a good start—try something more detailed: "I really appreciated the way that you rallied round when I lost my passport."

- **It is often heard loudest when least expected.** For example, on a car trip a couple of weeks later: "I know that you hate hospitals so it was really nice of you to come and visit my mother with me." This makes us feel our kindness has not been forgotten and therefore we feel doubly acknowledged.

- **It identifies unspoken feelings.** In difficult situations, communication can be improved by acknowledging the feelings behind the words or the mood. "I guess you're angry?" or "Are you sad?" Don't worry if you do not guess correctly, because your friend, date, or colleague will be happy to provide the correct emotion and instead of lurking unexpressed all the feelings will have been acknowledged.

## SUMMING UP

With ingrained or difficult problems, a couple can be like two people on a seesaw. The more one partner pushes down on their end, the more the second partner will shoot up in the air. The best way to come closer to each other is to move into the middle. Unfortunately, many people cannot hear the extent or the cause of their partner's unhappiness because they are frightened. However, improving communication can resolve even the toughest problem and save the day.

## IN A NUTSHELL:

- Little changes improve the overall atmosphere in a relationship and put down the foundations for big changes.

- By relaxing your stance on a contentious issue, it will allow your partner to relax hers or his.

- Acknowledging the full extent of your problems can be the first step to turning around your relationship.

# CHAPTER TWELVE

# Coming Back From Crisis Point

How do I know when it's time to throw in the towel and stop trying to rescue my marriage? That's a question I'm asked over and over again. I have one simple answer: When you've tried everything and you're still stuck. Unfortunately, most people have tried the same failed strategy over and over again. I hope that the love hacks in this book have provided some inspiration for other ideas to try. Next, I'm going to look specifically at couples whose relationship has reached the make or break point. I've divided the chapter into two sections. The first part is aimed at the person initiating the crisis and the second at someone reacting to one. Please read both sections, partly for the insight into how your partner might be feeling, but mainly because there are more similarities than differences between the two positions than you might imagine.

## INITIATING THE CRISIS

For most people the crisis has been a long time coming. Over the years, they have tried to communicate their unhappiness, boredom, or frustration and although there might have been a few attempts to "try harder" nothing has really changed. Couples can jog along in "OK" mode for quite some time until a trigger point comes along and everything changes.

Tania, twenty-seven, had been living with her partner for eighteen months when a new arrival at work turned her life upside down. She wrote to my website: "I'm utterly confused because no bodily fluids have been exchanged—not even a kiss. I've tried to ignore these feelings and distract myself with other projects—I baked all today. But I've been more fulfilled by my work colleague's written words and voice; even though I've never even shed clothes with him, I suddenly know that my partner has been going about things in the bedroom all wrong. So I've avoided coming to bed until my partner's asleep and I hate being kissed by him. I feel sexy and desired on one hand and like a duplicitous monster on the other." Fortunately the colleague was on a three-week secondment to Tania's division, so she did not act on her impulses but it was a wake-up call. "How could I have allowed my relationship to decay to such an extent that I allowed someone else in?"

When Shelby returned home from dropping off her daughter at university—along with twenty boxes of her belongings—her heart sank: "I walked back through the door and Spencer hardly looked up from the television. I wanted to tell him about her room and how I felt waving her goodbye but he was more interested in baseball." Their problems went back a long way. "He'd always been a homebody and didn't like socializing. I'm more outgoing except I didn't mind so much when the children were young because the house was always full of noise and activity, but over the past few years trouble had been brewing. Finally, I knew something had to change. I couldn't sit beside him on the couch. So I turned around and went out for a walk, to clear my head, build up my courage. I had to break free or something would die inside."

Sean's forty-second birthday party prompted his turning point: "I've been ground down by a long commute, stress at work and home—at both places I feel taken for granted. I've been crying a lot, wanting a cuddle but not sex, and basically my feelings have been all over the place. My wife organized this wonderful party but I just didn't want to be there." Six months earlier Sean's father had died: "It's a real reminder that we're not here forever. Life's too short to be miserable or to feel this alone."

Everybody reaches crisis point in a different way, but the impulse is the same: Something must be done. Unfortunately many people have no clear idea what that "something" should be and little idea how to communicate effectively with their partner.

If this sounds familiar, how can you move forward? How do you explain your feelings to your partner? What if he or she is unlikely to cooperate?

## Difficult People

Although I believe that "people are OK," some partners are difficult and won't participate in solving relationship problems. In some cases, they are lost to drink, drugs, or a violent temper and therefore unavailable for a relationship. In these circumstances, you should ask yourself if it is wise to stay in this relationship.

If your relationship is fairly new—less than eighteen months old—it could be that your partner is "OK" for someone else but not the man or woman for you.

However, in the majority of cases, if your partner is "difficult," it is because he or she is frightened and finds it harder to listen. The road ahead will be daunting but there is no reason why your relationship cannot be saved. However, it is important to find the right way of communicating. Your strategy should depend on whether your partner makes decisions based largely on intuition or rational thought.

**Sensers:** These are practical or rational people who are most likely to be swayed by facts and figures. They downplay emotions and favor a "common-sense" approach.

When Spencer's wife, Shelby, told him she was unhappy, he couldn't understand the problem: "You've got a lovely house, everything that you could want. No shortage of money."

Like many Sensers, Spencer concentrated on what was happening today and dismissed any past grievances. So when Shelby complained about never going out, he replied: "But you never said anything at the time, and anyway I can't change the past." Logically, he was right, but this only made Shelby more frustrated.

Sensers will also try to shut down an argument by concentrating on their partner's personal issues rather than accept any problems with their relationship. Indeed, Spencer told Shelby: "I'm not stopping you going out more."

Perhaps unsurprisingly, Shelby got angry and stormed out. However, Spencer was not being difficult or dismissive. He genuinely could not understand her viewpoint, mainly because his way of processing information was entirely different.

**Intuitors:** These are instinctive people who are swayed more by feelings rather than argument. They are less concerned about practical matters (such as money or where to live) and more focused on abstract concepts (such as fulfillment, reaching their potential, or being "in love"). While Sensers are thoughtful, Intuitors speak first and think about other's reactions afterward.

When Sean, who had a crisis after his forty-second birthday, told his wife, Madeleine, that he was unhappy and lacked direction, she exploded: "After everything I've done, you come to me with some half-baked story. You don't love me and …"

Sean interrupted the torrent: "I didn't say that."

"All those years when I thought you were happy, that we were happy. All ruined."

Intuitors tend to wrap the past into the present because, in their mind, yesterday's good times have been polluted by today's issues.

In contrast with Sensers, who take little or no responsibility for the problem, Intuitors—like Madeleine—take more than their share and often feel totally to blame.

Not surprisingly, Intuitors overreact, in stark contrast to Sensers who downplay any problem.

## What to Say and What Not to Say

Whether your partner is a Senser or an Intuitor, please don't deliver an ultimatum. This will only create panic, start a ticking clock (where none needs to exist), and make it harder for your partner to hear your core message.

## Dealing with a Senser

🌱 Keep your explanation simple.

🌱 Take responsibility for any personal dissatisfaction and explain what steps you are taking to remedy it.

🌱 Explain what is making you unhappy in the relationship—placing the emphasis on today's problems.

🌱 Avoid examples from the past, even if they illustrate the point or are connected to present issues, as your partner is likely to switch off.

🌱 Back up your abstract goals (like more excitement) with concrete examples (such as a trip to India).

🌱 Stress value and the financial savings of your solution.

🌱 Keep calm and don't overburden your partner by getting emotional.

## Dealing with an Intuitor

🌱 Keep your explanation simple.

🌱 Take responsibility for any personal dissatisfaction and explain what steps you will take to remedy it.

🌱 Tell your partner what you value about her or him.

🌱 Explain what is making you unhappy in the relationship, being clear about when the problems started (and your happiness before that point).

🌱 Listen to your partner and acknowledge any anger, tears, or upset. Until she or he has drained their feelings, they are unlikely to be ready to truly listen.

🌱 Keep calm.

## Keep Going Forward

The aftermath of a confession about how unhappy you've been is always stressful and uncomfortable. The best way of dealing with the fallout, once again, depends on how your partner processes difficult situations.

If your partner is a Senser, he or she might have listened but not seemed to register the conversation. The temptation is to threaten a divorce, but before you escalate matters, try writing a letter or an email. Putting your thoughts in writing gives your partner a chance to think through both your complaints and why he or she might have fallen into this trap. Here is a letter to my website, from Desmond, prompted by his partner sending him just such an email:

> "I have been married for nine years and I have never been a true father, nor a husband. I've never helped around the house, cleaned up, or done chores. It took my wife emailing me a detailed list of my faults for me to realize what I needed to be. I'd thought that just being here I was a better father than my Dad—who divorced my mom when I was young and was never there for me—but I neglected my children to play computer games, to go fishing, or do the things I loved. I thought that because my wife didn't work, it was kind of her duty to do everything at home. I made her feel more like a maid than a wife."
>
> In this email, she told me this was my last chance to be the husband and father she knew I could be. So I have now stepped up and started working on becoming that person. I am busting my butt off taking care of work, the kids, her, the house and anything else I can do to take some of the load off her."

So why should writing bring about such a huge change of attitude? Having read the original email to Desmond from his wife, I would make the following points. It was not too long (about 800 words). The tone was friendly ("I hope you had a wonderful day fishing"). It gave credit where it was due ("I'm thankful for the last nine years, you have been a great provider and allowed me the opportunity to stay home with the children" and "hearing I love you is great but you need to show us as well"). There were no threats and she did not diagnose Desmond's problems—which can get people's backs up—thereby allowing him to draw the conclusions about his father for himself. Finally, her complaints were specific and backed up with an example.

If your partner is an Intuitor, you might be tempted to back-pedal or feel overwhelmed and hopeless—but don't give up. Revealing the depth of your unhappiness will have changed the dynamics of your relationship and created a willingness to look deeper.

Malcolm and Ruth, both in their early fifties, had been living together for nearly thirty years and had a child together but they had not married. Although there had been good times, Ruth had not felt truly loved over the past five years. When she initiated the crisis that brought them into counseling, she told Malcolm: "I have never felt sure of you—right from the beginning you could not commit to me. I sort of understood because I'd come out of a long-term relationship and didn't want to fall in love either." They had been students on an overland bus exploring Europe and Asia. "But I couldn't understand why you shut me out and wanted to go off sightseeing with the others," she continued, "because I loved you so much and always wanted to be with you."

It was Malcolm's turn to speak: "You keep using your overwhelming love as an excuse for being demanding. You can't see that it's like a form of abuse. You stop me from going off and doing the things that interest me." They were already well aware of pattern of Ruth clasping Malcolm tight and him wriggling away. However, Ruth's declaration that they sorted this problem out or called it a day provided the focus to start facing the central "unsayable" issue in their relationship—how to balance individual space and couple togetherness—and finally begin to resolve it.

Whether your partner is a Senser or an Intuitor, it is worth remembering the lessons of Chapter Ten and valuing the benefits of how your partner approaches a problem. A good decision needs the cool head of the Senser (who weighs up all the evidence) and the emotional intelligence of the Intuitor (who listens to any messages from the unconscious). If you can work together to solve your relationship's underlying problems, you have the makings of a good team.

Finally, if you have been suppressing the seriousness of your relationship problems for quite some time, it is likely that you will be feeling depressed. The following exercise will help you find enough energy to keep going forward.

## BEAT THE BLUES

The blues kick in whenever we feel overwhelmed by helplessness. This is why even something very minor, but empowering, can help us break out.

- Set up small triumphs and easy successes. For example, tackling a nasty chore that you have delayed for ages–such as sorting out the cupboard under the sink. Afterward, these jobs will provide a real sense of achievement.

- Find small boosts to your self-image. On the weekend, make certain that you get dressed rather than hanging around in your dressing gown, or splash out on some new clothes.

- Help other people. Offering to fix the guttering for an elderly neighbor or volunteering for the girl guides' camp will not only divert your attention from your own problems but their praise and thanks will make you feel better about yourself.

- Compare yourself to someone worse off. Cancer patients often reassure themselves by comparing themselves to someone sicker. Next time you find yourself wishing your life was like that of a lucky friend, try being thankful it is not like someone much less fortunate than you.

- Take up yoga, swimming, or some form exercise as the natural endorphins lift spirits, help relaxation, and take your mind off worries.

- If you are religious, try praying; if not, look for a meditation class. These are often run by local Buddhist centers. They will not look to convert, but rather teach you to empty your mind. It is a hard goal, but even getting a few moments peace from an overactive brain can be very uplifting.

# HOW TO GET YOUR LOVER BACK

If your partner has dropped the bombshell that she or he is seriously unhappy or is threatening to break up your relationship, you will probably still be reeling from the shock. So try not to panic, make a snap decision, or expect to solve the problems overnight. It will take time and contemplation, but the following advice will significantly improve your chances of success.

## Acknowledge Your Partner's Message

Your partner will probably say some shocking and hurtful things. It is natural to want to defend yourself or put the record straight. However, this will probably prompt a row, sound like you are making excuses, and prevent your partner from recognizing that you have truly heard her or him.

Instead, acknowledge your partner's message by repeating back the key items. For example: "You've been unhappy for years and feel taken for granted." (Don't worry if you are stressed and might not have heard everything properly, your partner will clarify, for example, "not 'taken for granted' but ignored.")

Keep asking questions, so you can be sure that you have properly understood. From time to time, summarize your partner's case back to him or her. This will help you check that you are neither downplaying nor exaggerating the situation.

Finally, when your partner is all talked out and feels heard—ask you if you're unclear—you can explain your position and feelings.

## Acknowledge Your Failings

Although it is tempting to present yourself in the best light possible, accepting justified criticism will build a rapport between you and your partner. It also shows that you have truly listened, accept there are problems in the relationship, and take your share of responsibility for what's gone wrong. Most importantly, acknowledging your failings will help build trust.

Kip Williams, a psychologist at the University of Toledo in Ohio, studied what happened when lawyers exposed a weakness in their case before the other team had a chance to point it out. Interestingly, the jurors rated the lawyers who confessed their failings as more trustworthy and, therefore, listened more carefully to their case.

To increase the power of this strategy, be specific. I often counsel people trying to save their marriage, who tell their partner: "I know I'm not perfect." Unfortunately, this sort of blanket acknowledgment seldom works as it fails to show an understanding of how their behavior impacted on their partner. A more effective approach would be: "I know I should have listened more" or "I should have tried harder."

So think about what you would like to do differently and talk over your findings with your partner.

## Take Responsibility for Your Failings

We imagine that blaming our problems on circumstances beyond our control will get us an easier ride. However, research suggests that it is best to own up and take responsibility.

Social scientist Fiona Lee studied the results of public-listed companies and found that those where company chairmen put the blame on something internal (and therefore under their control) rather than external (like the global market, weather, or economy) had higher stock prices one year later. Why should this be? Lee believes that companies that took responsibility were considered by stockholders to have diagnosed the problems and were attending to them. Meanwhile, the companies that blamed forces out of their control appeared helpless and hapless.

So how do you use this research? Instead of blaming "pressure of work" or "the children eating up all the time"—which are eternal problems—take responsibility: "I didn't prioritize home life" or "I need to make certain we can have time away together." This will show your partner that you're willing to act as a team to resolve the underlying problems.

Finally, use this strategy sparingly. Don't go overboard and take all the responsibility for the crisis; good communication is a joint responsibility. In addition, one or two failings build trust, a long list sounds hopeless.

## Get a Personal Recommendation

On one hand, you don't want to talk about your strengths, achievements, and the goodness of your character as this would sound boastful. Yet on the other hand, it is important to remind your partner that although the relationship might appear broken, you still have many positive qualities.

Get round this quandary by asking someone close to sing your praises. It does not matter if the personal recommendation comes from your mother—who is bound to praise—or another member of your family.

However, don't involve your children as you don't want to alarm them. The other warning is to use this strategy sparingly. One recommendation reminds your partner of your good qualities. Several can sound like an attempt at brainwashing and turn him or her off.

## Collaborate

When it comes to solving a crisis, many heads are better than one. However, think through who you will recruit to help. Although it is nice to have people cheering you on, someone who can see both sides of the argument or who is willing to point out where you are going wrong is far more valuable. So look for a team who can offer support, a sounding board, and knowledge of the road ahead.

The good news is that by reading this book, you've already embraced the importance of collaborating. So let's think back over some of things you have learned about communication: "I can ask, you can say no, and we can negotiate." When you are stressed, you are likely to fall back into old habits, so be careful. If you are tempted to interrupt your partner, and not properly listen, try biting the inside of your cheek. Don't forget the importance of small changes, which are repeated and become habits. For example, eating together, sending loving texts, and giving compliments. Finally, I always suggest giving your partner the benefit of the doubt and not jumping to conclusions, which may be wrong (see the next exercise).

If you are seeking to nudge your partner into giving your relationship a second chance, the next exercise is particularly effective.

## EXERCISE   LABELING

We are always assigning traits, attitudes, beliefs, and labels to other people. This is why airlines use announcements on arrival such as: "We know you have many airlines to choose from, so we thank you for choosing to fly with us." It sends all sorts of subtle messages. Firstly, the announcement reminds you that you have chosen them. Secondly, it confirms your confidence in your choice—after all, you've landed safely and on time. Without any cost, and with minimum effort, they have labeled themselves as a great company. How can you use this knowledge to persuade your partner?

1. **Check the labels that you are giving your partner.** Continually and anxiously asking your partner "How are you feeling?," "Any changes?," "Should we talk about our situation?" just labels the relationship as "in crisis." Worse still, by labeling your partner as someone "about to leave," you could turn your fears into a self-fulfilling prophesy.

2. **Give your partner a positive label.** Alternatives include: "You're a reasonable person" or "We've always tried to make decisions together" or "I know you don't want to hurt me." Obviously, these have to come from the heart and be genuinely credible, so your partner recognizes him or herself.

3. **Make a request in keeping with this label.** For example, "I know you don't want to hurt me, so I'd be grateful if you could come to counseling with me" or "You're a reasonable person, so I hope you'll tell me if ..."

---

# DEALING WITH CRITICISM, REJECTION, AND SETBACKS

In an ideal world, your partner will notice your determination to change and support the process. Unfortunately, she or he will be angry or fed up after years of working alone on the relationship and therefore highly skeptical. So instead of cooperation, you are likely to face obstacles and stonewalling, but don't despair. Here are the most common problems, the possible pitfalls, and some effective fight-back strategies.

## "My Partner Is Not Only Critical but Sometimes Downright Nasty"

It is tough enough dealing with a negative partner but quite another thing to deal with someone whose criticism has become personal.

After spending seven years together and having two children, Edward and Adrienne had hit a wall in their marriage. Adrienne complained that there was no "connection" between them and was adamant that they should split. She agreed to come to counseling only because Edward begged. When I asked how things had been at home, Edward complained that Adrienne's behavior toward him had been: "Horrible, bordering on hate and a lot of resentment." He was puzzled and unable to understand why trying to save his marriage should be greeted with such a response.

However, there are always two sides to an argument. Adrienne sat in the chair opposite silently fuming. So I asked Edward if he had done anything to justify this reaction? "I'd taken the kids for a weekend away—it had originally been planned as a break for me and Adrienne but she refused to come, so my mom came instead. We all had a wonderful time together, although I had an empty ache inside, but I did my best to ignore it. When we returned all happy, Adrienne said something that triggered something inside me and I flew off the handle and shouted at her and said hurtful things for which I later apologized."

Adrienne finally spoke: "Tell him what you called me."

Edward shook his head.

"He called me a 'bitch' and a whole lot worse. He says he loves me, he wants to make the relationship work, and that's how he behaves."

"That was completely wrong and I did apologize." Edward obviously imagined that this wiped the slate clean.

Meanwhile, Adrienne sunk back into silence.

**Worst mistake:** Fighting fire with fire. However much you feel justified in losing your temper and ranting, your partner will just view your outburst as proof that the relationship is fundamentally flawed.

**Fight-back strategy:** Acknowledge your partner's feelings—for example, "I can see that you're angry." Although this might encourage your partner to off-load—which could be unpleasant—it is better than trying to dam or divert her or his feelings. However much you are provoked by what you hear, keep calm, and then report your own feelings.

## "Nothing I Do Seems to Make Any Difference"

When your partner unilaterally declares that your marriage is over, the pain is overwhelming. One half of your brain can't believe it's happening and the other is trying to fix the mess as quickly as possible. It is almost as if you're looking for a magic solution to make everything all right again.

"I stumbled across a photo of us both looking happy from last summer," said Edward on his first solo counseling session—Adrienne had refused to continue. "So I had this idea and put together a mini album of good moments and a letter, not asking her to stay, but explaining how I feel, and mailed them with a CD of two songs that I sang. I hope it will be a pleasant surprise and she doesn't see it as desperate, and that they invoke some emotion in her like they did me. I suspect it will have the opposite effect, but I am running out of options."

**Worst mistake:** Becoming so fixated on your magic solution that you're blind to the bigger picture. Meanwhile your partner cannot understand why, when the marital ship is sinking, you are so preoccupied with rearranging the deck chairs. When your efforts, such as going for one counseling session, arranging a romantic trip to Paris, or spending a family Christmas together, don't have the desired effect, the likelihood is that you will explode or sink into depression.

**Fight-back strategy:** When people claim to have tried everything, what they mean is that they've tried every ingenious trick to "magic" their marriage back to health. However, they have not tried listening to their partner—truly listening. By this I mean, imagining that everything your partner says is true (just for a minute) and imagining how he or she must be feeling. Standing in your partner's shoes, however temporarily, will help you begin to address the real issues.

## "My Partner Is Shutting Down Her or His Feelings"

After the initial declaration that a relationship is in crisis, couples do a lot of talking. Quite often these discussions go round in circles—normally because each partner has diametrically opposed opinions. There might be the occasional optimistic sign—like the initiator buys flowers or sends a caring text—but slowly the mood becomes darker and darker until communication grinds to a halt. So what's going on? There are three possible scenarios.

Firstly, the initiator feels it is pointless trying to explain anymore because his or her partner will never "get it." This could be because he or she is too upset to hear, contradicts everything, or simply shouts down all opposition.

Secondly, the initiator finds it hard to understand the situation him or herself; she or he is fed up with going through the daily motions, wants more out of life but can't really explain what. In most cases, the initiator is going through some form of midlife crisis or sliding into depression. (I have written more on these topics in my book: *It's Not a Midlife Crisis, It's an Opportunity: How to forty- and fifty-something without going off the rails*.)

Finally, the initiator is keeping something back. When Edward finally learned to listen to Adrienne, she admitted that she'd been speaking to an old flame behind his back. "She says she has feelings for him but she doesn't know what those feelings are," he explained at his third solo session. Sometimes there is a full-blown affair, but usually a friend or work colleague is becoming more than "just a good friend." Edward was in despair: "Why didn't she tell me?" The initiator can be simply ashamed of her or his behavior. However, more often, they consider the "friendship" to be a side issue (a symptom of the problem, not the cause) but suspect their partner will zero in on this other person and blame everything on them.

**Worst mistake:** Thinking it will all blow over. When everything goes quiet, or the initiator stops complaining, the partner trying to save the relationship manages to convince him or herself that things are getting better. On the surface this might be true, but the initiator is either preparing their exit or distracting themselves with a self-medication affair.

**Fight-back strategy:** Sometimes things have to get worse to get any better. Although the truth might hurt, at least all the problems are in the open and can finally be addressed. Keep calm and don't be distracted from the real issues.

## "I Feel Like I'm Wasting My Time"

Once you have reached this scenario, the situation is indeed bleak.

Your partner is no longer spiteful or nasty—which should make you feel better—but being ignored or seen as irrelevant is worse. The hours spent going round and round the same old subjects were draining and depressing, but at least you were talking.

When Edward arrived for his fourth session, he sounded defeated, deflated, and dejected. "I persuaded her to explain what she wants from life and she listed five things—own her own house, a stable family life for the children, a career when the children go back to school, be in a loving happy relationship, and I can't remember the fifth. But she has all those things now and all the freedom she desires. Yet if we split, we will both be basically on the breadline for the foreseeable future; she admitted that it will set her back five to ten years." He took his head out of his hands. "I feel we do have the 'happy, loving relationship,' but she says we don't have the emotional connection and the physical relationship. Our relationship is deeper than that and we have many, many other important connections—such as the children. Yet she seems hell-bent on achieving this fairy-tale love." It was a classic sense versus intuitive debate but instead of engaging with the arguments on a deeper level, Edward was about to throw in the towel. He had not stopped loving his wife but wondered if giving up, attempting to switch off his feelings, or "seeing other people" would make him feel better.

**Worst mistake:** Begging for another chance or making empty promises. This is not only a sure sign that you have not been listening to your partner—even though he or she has been trying to communicate in increasingly negative ways—but offers no plausible vision of how your relationship could improve. Worse still, begging destroys your self-esteem and forfeits any lingering respect from your partner.

**Fight-back strategy:** Instead of waiting for a sign that the relationship is "not beyond hope" or pushing for an agreement to "try again," take the initiative and start working on the relationship yourself. Understand what went wrong, think about the changes you'd like to make and start to implement them. Who is most likely to spark your partner's interest again: someone getting on with their life and doing interesting things or someone mired in bitterness and forever bringing up old grievances?

## WHAT DO I REALLY WANT?

Whether you are the person initiating a crisis or the person reacting to one, it is important to have a clear idea of your goal. It will give you something to cling on to during the difficult weeks ahead and improve communication with your partner. Unfortunately, many people find it hard to articulate what they want.

Bella, from Chapter Ten, whose husband was unhappy but couldn't decide whether he wanted to stay and work on the relationship or leave, found this task particularly difficult: "But it's not what I want, everything is down to Jeff. I'm just waiting for him to make his mind up."

"Except, there are two of you in this relationship," I replied, "and what you want has to count too. Imagine that I have a magic wand under my chair, what would you wish for?"

Bella was silent.

"It's a magic wand, so you can have anything."

Finally, she replied: "I want him to love me back."

I wrote her statement on a flip chart in large letters, as writing down a key goal not only makes it more real but fixes it in the front of our mind. There were tears in Bella's eyes. "Why was that so hard to say?" I asked.

"I don't want to be rejected again."

Like many people in her situation, Bella was fighting for her marriage with one hand but holding back with the other—frightened of getting hurt. Not only did this behavior cut her firepower by half, it sends out a mixed message. Bella immediately recognized this trap.

"One moment, I'm telling him he doesn't have to sleep on the couch and inviting him to bed and making love, but the next I'm angry and sending him back downstairs."

"And what would happen if he did reject you?" I asked.

"I would just have to get on with it," she said. This time, there were no tears or upset—just total calmness.

In effect, Bella had looked calmly at her greatest fear and knew if the worst came to the worst, she could cope. She left the session feeling not only better but more in charge of her future.

Although it might seem dangerous to admit out loud what you want, I believe it is always best to fight for your heart's desire and lose than to give up without a struggle. So if you are coping with the fallout from your partner's declaration of unhappiness, don't wait for a sign or some encouragement from him or her to make your wish come true. Write it down and turn it into your mission statement through the difficult months ahead.

At first sight, the partner initiating the crisis should find it easier to explain their goal. Unfortunately, it often comes out as what they don't want rather than what they do. When I asked Sean, whose crisis started at his forty-second birthday party, for his goals, he replied: "I don't want to be like my father, always doing what other people expect" and "to break out of this rut." Knowing what he wished to avoid was fine but it did not bring Sean any closer to changing his life. When I asked him to imagine a magic wand, he said: "I want to travel" and "I want more responsibility at work." By framing his goal as a positive, rather than a negative, he could immediately think of some steps to turn his dream into a reality.

Whichever side of the crisis divide you're standing, there is one word that will make it easier to communicate your goal to your partner. That word is "because." There are two reasons why "because" is so powerful: it explains and it contains.

Taking Bella as an example, she told Jeff: "I want you to love me back because ... through all this upheaval I've discovered the depth of my feelings for you. Beforehand, I'd really just been going through the motions." She had explained why she wanted the relationship to continue and contained Jeff's imagination by heading off any possible alternative conclusions—such as wanting to stay together for the sake of the children, saving money, or keeping up appearances.

In Sean's case, he told Madeleine: "I want to travel because … I never got the chance when I was younger. I went off to university and got stuck into a job." This explained his feeling of missing out but contained Madeleine's fears—for example, that he wanted to get away from her.

## EXERCISE   THE "RIGHT TRAP"

When a couple is in conflict, and the arguments get nasty, both partners are quick to cloak themselves in righteousness. However "being right" is a trap. It casts your partner as "wrong," part of the problem, and therefore "deserving" of your anger, bitterness, and frustration. Worse still, your partner is defending her or his unpleasant behavior by using just the same defense of being "right." So break this destructive cycle by using the following exercise:

- After a row, instead of pumping up your anger by going over all the points where you were in the "right" and your partner was "wrong," close your eyes and imagine that you are walking through the jungle when the ground suddenly gives way.

- You have fallen into the "Right Trap"—a deep, dark pit that has been camouflaged by a few innocent-looking sticks (day-to-day issues) that don't seem threatening but easily break.

- Imagine looking round the pit, in your mind, and think about all the things that you have been "right" about: how might your partner think she or he is "right" on those issues too?

- If you cannot imagine your partner being "right" about these specific circumstances, pan back—like a camera—and reveal more of the past days, months, and years: Are there reasons from your wider life together why she or he might feel "right" on this issue?

- Ask yourself: is being right getting me anywhere?

- Ultimately, there is your "right" and your partner's "right" and probably if a hundred different people were polled on the same circumstances, they would come up with countless more "rights."

- So climb out of the "Right Trap" by no longer discussing your marital problems with friends—who will side with you and reinforce your belief that your interpretation is the only "right" one.

- Finally, imagine standing outside the "Right Trap" and feeling how good it is to be up in the light again, able to see your partner's viewpoint too.

---

# MOVING FORWARD

Whether you are the person who has initiated the crisis or the person reacting to one, if you have acknowledged your partner's feelings, truly listened, and accepted that there needs to be changes, the atmosphere should be much more positive. But how do you keep building on these changes?

## Concentrate on How Far You've Come

It is easy to be daunted by the scale of the task of rescuing your relationship. So look at what you have achieved already—especially as the first steps are the hardest—rather than what still needs to be done. Strangely enough, the last part of the journey will be the most straightforward. This is because the closer we are to achieving our goal, the more confident we feel and therefore the harder we push to achieve it.

## Focus on the Changes You'd Like

When things are going badly, it is nearly always because one or both of you have slipped back into old ways and either stopped communicating effectively or communicated only negatives. So refocus on what works and find positive short-term goals to make your relationship better.

## Give Yourself Time

In the same way that a relationship deteriorates slowly over months and years of disappointment, it takes time to rebuild trust again. So don't expect results too quickly; both parties will need solid evidence that any changes are lasting and that the gains will not slip away. Ultimately, you will need both patience and persistence.

I often see people who possess one of these qualities but not the other. Persistence alone is a problem as it can easily become demanding, anxious, and dissatisfied. Patience alone is also a problem. The risk is that nothing changes or someone minimizes their needs and always puts other's first—until they become resentful and angry. However, the golden combination of patience and persistence is nearly always rewarded with a greatly improved relationship.

# THE LONG PICTURE

Sometimes the odds are so stacked against a relationship that separation is the only answer. However, a temporary split does not necessarily have to become permanent. Chelsea's forty-seven-year-old husband announced that he had fallen in love at a distance with a colleague (who was almost oblivious to his feelings), bought an apartment, and threatened to move in. At that point, Chelsea had little hope and felt "sick with misery."

Her husband did leave but when nothing happened with his colleague, not even a kiss, he started a passionate affair with a second colleague that lasted around four months. Despite her hurt, Chelsea kept the lines of communication open: "Throughout the year, he has been visiting me and our daughters (now ten and twelve) every second weekend or usually more frequently and stays over in the spare room. He phones nightly to speak to the children but he always talks to me too."

One year after the split, there seemed to be a window of opportunity to try again after Chelsea's husband split with his girlfriend: "We have a lot to talk about in the sense of books, movies, gossip, and other mutual interests. We have lots of laughs and give each other a kiss and hug goodnight. I certainly have to have this affectionate connection because if it wasn't there, my feelings would soon turn to total resentment and hate."

Chelsea had used the time apart to take up her profession again, get individual counseling, and work on herself: "I no longer have any cause to moan boringly about work and in public am pretty much the happy and feisty person I was when we met twenty-three years ago—except for being lovelorn, sad, and angry when alone. My friends admire my generosity and say 'hang on in there.' Could we find our relationship again or is it just fantasy?"

As in many cases where the relationship was basically sound but suddenly imploded, Chelsea's husband seemed to have suffered some form of midlife crisis—where everything in his old life no longer made sense and escape into a fantasy relationship seemed the only solution. Once someone in this situation has calmed down, taken stock, and realized that an exploratory affair has made their life worse rather than better, there is nearly always a chance to try again when the affair self-destructs.

If there is a window of opportunity for a second chance, how can you seize the moment? First of all, avoid talking about "The Future" as this will sound like an immensely scary project. Instead, discuss "going on a few dates" or "getting to know each other again."

Your partner will be worried about "leading you on" or "hurting you again." So bring these fears into the open and let him or her talk. However, stress that you are an adult and take responsibility for your own feelings and choices. Your partner does not need to "protect" you. You are an adult going into this with your eyes open—not a child that's been promised a pony!

Chelsea's husband was indeed worried and told her: "I don't know if I can have sex with you again." I helped her keep both his and her anxiety down by framing everything over the next few days. So

Chelsea told him: "I'm only asking if you'd like to go to the movies, not inviting you into my bed."

Many partners who are considering returning are worried about "spoiling the friendship." If this is the case, I think it is important to be honest and tell your partner that you will be upset in the short term but your number one priority will remain being the best possible parent for your children (and how that means still cooperating with each other).

## Coping During the Long Picture

If you and your partner are currently having "time apart" and you're considering playing the long game, it is important to focus on the following:

🌱 Work on yourself and healing your pain (rather than relying on your partner to return and make everything better.) I explain more in my book *Wake Up and Change Your Life: How to survive a crisis and be stronger, wiser and happier.*

🌱 Keep the children out of your marital problems. Although it will be hard, protect them from worst of your pain or they will feel duty-bound to side with you.

🌱 Step back and stop analyzing. Don't try to second-guess the meaning behind your partner's behavior or ask friends for reports of his or her feelings. Someone in crisis can experience everything from euphoria to despair in one day, so even if you do guess the correct feeling, another will be along shortly.

🌱 Understand what went wrong and what changes need to be made (either for trying again with your partner or to avoid making the same mistakes with someone new).

🌱 Review at six months and a year.

## SUMMING UP

Whichever side of the crisis divide you are standing, remove any "ticking clock"—a sense that everything must be sorted immediately. Understand why communication has been a problem and whether you put more stress on rational thought (Senser) or feelings (Intuitor). Check you are giving a clear message to your partner and don't expect a result overnight.

---

### IN A NUTSHELL:

- Think clearly about your main goal and how to communicate it consistently. Make certain that your words and actions match.

- Put yourself in your partner's shoes and try seeing the situation from her or his position.

- Instead of trying to second-guess your partner's state of mind, try asking a direct question about her or his feelings.

---

# CHAPTER THIRTEEN

---

# How to Move On

**W**hether you and your partner have been to the edge of sanity and back or just had a nasty row, it is important to learn lessons. Why did you reach this place? What could each of you do differently? What would make it easier to disagree in a healthy way next time round? This final chapter has love hacks to help with this goal, how to forgive each other, and how to repair any damage done to your relationship.

## HOW TO POSTMORTEM A PAINFUL ARGUMENT

Although it is useful to go over the buildup to a row and the issues covered—to identify what helped and what hindered—examining the language used is even more beneficial. Time and again, how a couple argue defines how likely they are to find a resolution and, most importantly, one that sticks. Below is a list of three kinds of language used in an argument. They range from positive at the top, through neutral in the middle, and negative at the bottom. During a row, it is likely that you will roam across the full range. What counts is where the majority of your language sits. With mainly negative talk, you are less likely to reach agreement. With mainly positive talk, the chances of avoiding a repeat row or hours of sulking are significantly improved.

## Positive

**Complimentary:** "That's a good point" or "I admire your devotion."

**Acknowledging:** "So what you're saying is ..." or "I can see that you're angry."

**Agreement:** "You're right about my boss" or "We both want ..."

**Solution Seeking:** "So how do we move forward?" or "Would it help if ....?" (This is very helpful but be wary of heading here too soon.)

**Constructive:** "This is what I would like." (It is important to be up-front and clear about your needs rather than hoping that your partner will guess or telling him or her what you don't want.)

## Neutral

**Inquiring:** "What do you think?" or "Why didn't you phone?"

**Checking:** "So what happened is ..." or "You're saying ..."

**Explanation:** "My boss gave me a pile of extra work" or "The bus didn't come."

## Negative

**Disagreement:** "I didn't say that ..." or "I don't want us to stay late." (With the second example, we're all entitled to our viewpoint but it is always better expressed as in a constructive manner: "I'd like to get home before midnight.")

**Excuse:** "We had a rush on at work ..." (these sentences start like an explanation but change midway) " ... so I couldn't phone." (They become an excuse by adding how you chose to react—especially if that choice is presented as inevitable. In most circumstances, we could have found time to call.)

**Complaining:** "Don't leave your dirty cup in the sink." (Still only mildly negative.)

**Mind-Reading:** "You don't want me to enjoy myself," or "I knew you wouldn't phone." (From here onward, this talk becomes increasingly destructive.)

**Dismissive:** "Sure, of course you meant to phone" or "Don't give me that nonsense." (This often involves sarcasm, put-downs, sniping, and muttering under the breath.)

**Critical:** "You only think about yourself" or "You're a killjoy." (Attacking the person, not the behavior.)

**Black and white:** "I shouldn't have to ask for a hug" or "I'd never do that." (This are statements which suggest "I'm right" and "you're wrong.")

**Self-critical:** "I'm not as good as you at talking" or "Why would anyone listen to me?"

**Hopeless:** "There's no point talking about it" or "Why do I bother?" (Although some of the preceding language seems more negative, this is the most destructive kind because it closes down the conversation.)

## EXERCISE "FLAGGING"

We are not always aware of how our comments are heard. If your partner had parents who put her or him down, she or he will be conditioned to expect negatives and might, therefore, hear criticism even when none was intended. To get an accurate picture of the impact of your discussion on your partner, try this exercise:

- **Make a set of three cards.** On the first put a tick (positive), on the second put a cross (negative), and on the last put a dash (neutral).

- **Give the cards to your partner and start to explain your case about a reasonably contentious topic.** As you talk, your partner listens and (without comment) holds up the relevant card.

- **When you get a cross, stop and try to rephrase your comment until you get either a dash or a tick.** If you can't translate a cross into something positive, just move on to an another point.

- **Afterward conduct a postmortem.** Why did something sound negative and how it could possibly be transformed into a positive? What have you learned about yourself? What have you learned about your partner?

- **Change over and let the person flagging have a turn talking.**

## HOW TO APOLOGIZE AND BE FORGIVEN

What if your argument has ended in a nasty standoff? Although it is common to need time to calm down and think through an argument, some couples can be sullen, distant, walking on egg shells, and uncommunicative for two or three days. Not only is this extremely unpleasant, but makes people fearful and likely to avoid future confrontations. My aim in counseling is to cut down the recovery time to a few hours.

So what hinders and what helps? Unhelpful strategies include trying to "buy off" your partner—for example, offering to make a cup of coffee, give a back massage, or being extra nice. Your partner will interpret this as not taking his or her feelings seriously. Trying to make a joke out of her or his mood or the argument will have a similar effect. Hoping for the best or waiting for your partner to soften are also pointless and do nothing to end the standoff. There are, however, two useful strategies. The first is an invitation to postmortem the row. If the timing is bad—perhaps you have guests arriving—make an appointment to talk. The second strategy is an apology, but it is more than just saying "sorry":

🌷 **Acknowledge your part in the standoff.** For example: I shouldn't have been so critical. (Don't offer an explanation as this could sound like a justification, an excuse, or even an invitation for round two.)

💗 **Hold yourself responsible for the consequences.** For example: I really hurt you.

💗 **Express sorrow.** For example: "I'm ashamed that I opened my mouth without thinking."

This will not only break the deadlock, but encourage your partner to make a similar apology, provide an opportunity to talk, and promote a better argument next time round.

## UNDERSTAND YOUR PATTERN

If you can understand the bigger picture, you can head off unnecessary arguments and focus your attention on solving the sources of long-running disputes. So look at the following exercises; the idea is to understand just how closely your actions and those of your partner are linked, so try to find as many examples as possible.

In the run-up to an argument:

| When my partner does: | I tend to: |
|---|---|
| a) | a) |
| b) | b) |
| c) | c) |

| When I: | My partner tends to: |
|---|---|
| a) | a) |
| b) | b) |
| c) | c) |

When I did this exercise with Megan, twenty-five, and Harvey, twenty-nine, she immediately put: "When Harvey goes all quiet, I tend to get anxious and worried."

"What else?" I asked.

"When Harvey is still quiet, I push and push until I lose my temper and shout."

If I had been working with Megan alone, she would have filled in what Harvey did in these two circumstances, but as Harvey was there I asked him. "When Megan loses her temper, I keep quiet so I don't make things worse."

"What else?" I asked?

"When I walk away, that makes her angrier and angrier," he confessed.

Such as in the famous argument about which came first, the chicken or the egg, it does not matter whether Megan's temper made Harvey withdraw or Harvey's silence made Megan angry.

Ultimately, arguments are not your fault or your partner's but the combination of the two of you.

The next exercise looks at our expectations of our partner—these are the hundreds of small services, attributes, or reactions that we require our partner to observe or possess—but in most cases, we have never spoken out loud.

What I expect from my partner ...............

Why? .............

Is it fair? ............

Could I do this myself? ..........

One of the sources of rows between Megan and Harvey was home improvement and household maintenance tasks. So when Megan did this exercise, she wrote down: "I expect my partner to fix things." She had never really thought why she expected this. However, when we looked at her childhood, her memories of her father seemed always to feature him with a toolbox in hand. Megan stopped for a second:

"I just thought that if Harvey really cared he'd make an effort."

"But is that fair?"

"Not really, he's not interested or particularly handy and just because my Dad did it, why should he?" Megan conceded.

Finally, we looked at the alternatives to arguing about home improvement. Megan could start fixing stuff herself (perhaps after some lessons from her dad) or pay someone else to do the job.

## ME AND MY SHADOW

Every family has its rules. Some of them are very explicit: "Wash your hands before sitting down at the table" or "Don't talk with your mouth full." The really important rules, however, are seldom stated directly but policed by disapproving looks, ominous silences, sarcastic put-downs, and ostracism. So we learn from an early age that some feelings, behavior, or desires are simply unacceptable. Because we want to be loved by our parents, grandparents, brothers, and sisters, we play along and try to follow the rules. Unfortunately, these "unacceptable" parts of our character do not simply disappear—because they are part of being human—so we suppress or hide them away. In many ways, they are our shadow—very much part of us but simply unacknowledged.

Here are some of these rules: Don't fail; don't get above yourself; don't be such a child; don't grow up; don't make too much fuss; don't feel; don't get angry; don't be cleverer than me; stop putting yourself first.

Sometimes the rules are expressed in an open, positive way. For example, "You're the pretty one" or "You're the brains" or "You're so helpful." However, there is an unspoken down side to that: you have to be pretty, brainy, or helpful to be loved. Meanwhile, the contrasting parts of your personality (sporty, frivolous, or irresponsible) disappear into the shadows.

So ask yourself the following questions:

1. What were the unspoken rules when I was growing up?

2. What were the taboo feelings?

3. What did I miss out on by keeping those parts of myself in the dark?

4. What impact has it had on my relationship?

5. What would happen if I brought my shadow out into the light?

6. What is my worst fear? (Try to be as explicit as possible)

7. How likely is this to happen?

## FOCUS ON MORE FUN TOGETHER

When I listen to many couples talk about their evenings and weekends together, it sounds like a round of jobs to be completed, children to be ferried around, and other obligations to be fulfilled. "I just can't settle if there are clothes in the dryer that should be folded or the kitchen counters haven't been wiped down," said Hilary, thirty-three. She was often exhausted and complained that her husband, Calvin, forty-five, didn't do enough to help: "He's always saying 'put that down' or 'it can wait' and wanting me to relax and watch television with him, which would be nice, but has he ever thought I wouldn't be rushing around so much if did his share?" We could have spent weeks negotiating what tasks, when, and how, but I sensed the issue was deeper. It was almost as if Hilary had a heavy heart and although more support might have helped it would never be enough to lighten her load.

So I tried a different approach: "What do you do for fun?" They looked blank and it took about twenty seconds for either of them to respond. I felt like I'd asked for directions to the moon. Finally, Hilary answered:

"We have friends round from time to time."

But Calvin interrupted: "Not for a long time."

"I go over to my sister's and we share a bottle of wine."

"I have an old school friend down in Devon and I go down there once a month for the fishing."

No wonder everything felt so heavy. Life was a round of work, chores, and getting by. There was no chance to relax, be carefree, and have the sort of fun that leaves you feeling lightheaded and giggly. So we focused on them having more fun together, rather than on more housework. Next week, the atmosphere in the room had been transformed.

"It was a lovely fall day and rather than working in the garden, we decided to go for a walk in the local park," said Calvin.

"I don't know what came over me, but he was off in a world of his own and I sneaked behind a tree and jumped out at him."

"Gave me the fright of my life."

"And you chased me and we kicked this pile of leaves at each other."

"Much better than raking them up at home."

"And we dammed that stream with sticks and fallen leaves."

"I hadn't done that since I was twelve," said Calvin.

"When we returned home, Calvin offered to make dinner and I sat down and read the paper."

With plenty goodwill floating around, Hilary didn't need to ask for help because Calvin had already offered. If you'd like to bring more fun into your relationship, follow these simple guidelines:

- Differentiate between urgent and important. (The leaves in Calvin and Hilary's garden did need to be raked at some point, but it was not urgent and therefore did not need to take precedence over everything else.)

- Set aside plenty of relaxing time together. (Intimacy and fun cannot just be ordered up. Calvin and Hilary needed unstructured time in the park to relax and reconnect before they could let go and indulge themselves.)

- Don't be afraid to play. (Private jokes and anything that leaves you breathless, sweaty, and dirty are almost guaranteed to bring out your inner child.)

🌿 You can be happy together, even if you can't solve all your problems. (Hilary and Calvin still needed to work on many other areas but having the right mindset had transformed their relationship.)

## GENERATE EVEN MORE GOODWILL

Here are five proven ways for increasing goodwill from your partner. Try doing one a day and you'll keep the marital therapist away!

🌿 Respond cheerfully to your partner's request.

🌿 Look for something that needs to be done and do it without being asked.

🌿 Give your partner a cuddle or a hug (without expecting it to lead to sex).

🌿 Come home with an unexpected small gift.

🌿 Compliment your partner in front of other people. (For example, "he is very generous" or "I admire how elegant she looks.")

## LOOK FOR THE THIRD WAY

The third way is another idea from politics and came out of former president Bill Clinton's attempt to position himself above the simple right/left split that had dominated politics since the Second World War, and to co-opt the best from each world view. So how does it work for loving relationships? If you relax the urgency of your own case and develop empathy for your partner's viewpoint, the atmosphere in the house is immediately depolarized. Out of the calmness, something wonderful emerges. It will take a little time, so don't expect an immediate result, but a third option (not your way and not your partner's way) will slowly emerge.

Margery had expected her husband Gregory to retire at sixty (as his company had a policy of not putting more money into staff's pensions when they reached this age). However, Gregory found his work rewarding and his employers were keen to retain his services. "I've always played second fiddle to that damn company," said Margery bitterly, "I dropped my career and followed him around the world and I thought this would finally be our time."

Gregory saw things differently: "I have a team and we're working on this big account at the moment and I can't let them down, and anyway I don't feel ready to retire."

"That's all well and good but I'm left twiddling my thumbs rather than enjoying doing things together."

They both had a valid case. So I decided to use the third way and see if another option beyond retirement or continuing working would emerge:

- 🌷 **Express empathy for each other's position.** Margery said: "I know you've always got a lot of satisfaction and your identity from your work." Gregory said: "We have great fun together; I want to spend time with you."

- 🌷 **State as objectively as possible your needs and why you feel like that.** Margery said: "I want some project or plan for our retirement." Meanwhile, Gregory said: "I have ambitions and responsibilities at work. I don't feel ready for slippers."

- 🌷 **What do you accept about your partner's position? (Remember you don't have to be in wholehearted agreement.)** Margery said: "I share your need for something more than slippers." Gregory said: "I would like to buy a house on a lake and renovate it together."

- 🌷 **What small step could you make to show goodwill and go some way to alleviating the situation.** The couple agreed to plan their weekends and vacations—rather than Gregory just flopping around the house and unwinding from work—and started researching possible places to buy a second home.

- 🌷 **Sit back and wait.** Margery looked into a second career—something interesting but which would not tie her to nine-to-five. Eventually, she decided to train as a teaching assistant. Gregory enjoyed their weekends so much he negotiated an extra day off every fortnight. Finally, instead of seeing their two positions as incompatible, Margery and Gregory began to understand how they could be complementary: they could both relax and enjoy life, plus seek new challenges.

## SWAP-OVER WEEKEND

To help you truly empathize with your partner, and help facilitate your own third way, why not try this idea:

- To gain a fresh insight into what it is like to be your partner, you take over his or her jobs for the weekend.

- Meanwhile, your partner takes on your role.

- So if you normally take the children swimming, your partner will do that task. If he or she cuts the grass or does the grocery shopping, then you take over.

- Try to recreate each other's weekends as much as possible. The more you swap, the greater the understanding.

- Look for things you take for granted and that are so second nature that you have never questioned them before—for example, who is responsible for initiating sex.

- At the end of the weekend, relax and talk about your experiences of being each other, the insights gained, and what you might do differently in the future.

## ACCEPT WHAT YOU CAN'T CHANGE

A musical comedy ran in New York at the end of the 1990s for over five thousand performances, and was subsequently performed all over the world; a lot of its success was down to its witty title: *I Love You, You're Perfect, Now Change.* Audiences responded so warmly because they immediately recognized the absurd truth about love. On one hand, we love our partner just the way he or she is, but on the other we'd love him or her a little bit more if only he'd or she'd ... (fill in your particular bugbear).

When Jessica brought Gary into counseling, her main complaint was about his moods: "He'll arrive home with such a long face that it pulls me right down." Gary was equally unhappy: "She's on my case all the time, 'would I like this,' 'what's the matter,' or 'cheer it up it'll never happen.'"

The situation had got worse since they had started a family and Jessica would pester Gary to play with his son: "I want Gary to enjoy being with him." Jessica's motives might have been good, but they were driving a wedge between them. It also sounded like she was coaching Gary. I wondered what message that might be giving him. Jessica looked thoughtful, but before she could answer, Gary chipped in:

"You are not quite good enough the way you are."

"How does that make you feel?" I asked.

"Unloved," he replied.

But what would happen if Jessica reframed her attitude to Gary's "moods" not as a problem but as a fact of life? (After all, Gary had often said: "I'm not always down, I just have one of those faces.") This is because a "problem," invites a solution. Whereas a "fact of life"—like some people are naturally more pessimistic—is something that has to be accommodated.

Jessica agreed to experiment and see what would happen if she stopped trying to manage Gary's moods and his relationship with their son. First of all, the atmosphere in the house lightened—as they were having fewer rows. Jessica admitted: "It was hard to hold back, I thought nothing would change if I didn't do something, but actually I'm not responsible for his feelings—only he can be." Secondly, Gary started playing more with his son: "I could join in when it felt right—such as when he wanted help with building a tower out of his bricks—rather than barging in."

By accepting what she couldn't change, Jessica had not only accepted Gary (in all his complexity) but allowed him to have a different attitude to bringing up children. Their son could also fully benefit from their differences. Jessica could be a proactive mother—and head off any potential problems—and Gary could stand back and give their son enough space to learn things for himself. There is another benefit. We need difference to keep love and sexual attraction alive. Otherwise there is a danger of becoming so alike—almost brother and sister—and all desire disappears. (There is more in my book *I Love You But I'm Not In Love With You.*)

Another example of reframing a "problem" as a "fact of life" is Maxine and Rosie—a lesbian couple in their thirties. Maxine wanted Rosie to give up smoking: "I hate the smell, what it does to her health, and when we're out shopping, if we stop for a coffee I have to sit outside in the cold if I want to talk to Rosie," said Maxine. She tried complaining, bribing, and persuading Rosie to cut down by rolling her own—all without success. In fact, she had tried everything beyond accepting that she couldn't change Rosie. It was hard not to drop hints, sigh, or get touchy when Rosie slipped out for a cigarette, but slowly but surely she accepted Rosie's smoking as a "fact of life." "She'd smoked when I first met her, so it's not like I didn't know—I just thought I could change her," Maxine laughed.

Interestingly, twelve months later, Rosie gave up smoking of her own accord. It is a pattern that I observe time and again; the moment we give up trying to change our partner—and accept him or her warts and all—is the moment our partner becomes ready to change.

If you're thinking of offering the gift of acceptance, tell your partner that "I would still like you to _____ (fill in the gap) but I realize that it's counterproductive to pressurize. So I'm going to stop dropping hints or trying to apply subtle pressure. It doesn't mean that I don't still want you to ... but it's up to you." It will take patience and persistence and you will have to bite your tongue occasionally. If you find yourself slipping, remember the Serenity Prayer attributed to American theologian Reinhold Niebuhr (1892–1971) and frequently used by Alcoholics Anonymous:

*God, grant me the serenity*
*To accept the things I cannot change,*
*The courage to change the things that I can,*
*And the wisdom to know the difference.*

## **EXERCISE** WHAT I APPRECIATE ABOUT MY PARTNER

Rather than worrying about what you don't have, think about what you do. Write down as many examples of what you appreciate about your partner as possible. Don't overlook the tasks that are so every day that they have become almost invisible—such as filling up the car with gas, putting out the trash, or buying toilet paper.

On an average weekday, my partner does the following for me:

On an average weekend, my partner does the following for me:

I admire the following qualities in my partner:

## GO BEYOND CYNICISM

For more and more people, the standard default position is cynicism. In many ways, this is not surprising. We live in an increasingly individualistic society—where everybody is encouraged to ask: "What's in it for me?" Celebrities and politicians are always being uncovered for saying one thing and doing another. On an average day, we see more than 3,500 brand images and are bombarded with messages that this or that product will bring fulfillment and happiness. No wonder it is not just political interviewers who are asking themselves: "Why is this lying bastard lying to me?"

However, for a relationship to flourish it is important to go beyond the cynicism of "all men are after just one thing" and "a clever woman knows how to get her own way," or "I'll scratch your back, if you'll scratch mine." Instead of expecting the worst, we need to move beyond gender stereotyping and look for the best in our partner. Rather than listening to the cynical background music of newspapers and television—and the cynical voice in our own head claiming "they would say that"—we need to embrace hope, compassion, and in particular, generosity.

Why is generosity so important? Instead of waiting passively for our partner to make the first move, or offer some sign or encouragement, we need to take control and act ourselves. It might take a generous spirit to give with no strings attached and no expectation of a return. However, when someone finds that level of generosity, it can completely turn a relationship round.

When Joanne was being courted by Sebastian, he seemed a great romantic. He'd written the most amazing letters and driven through the night to be with her. But after the wedding everything changed. "He wasn't telling me that he loved me anymore and he was spending more and more time in the garage on his bikes or his collection of antique pocket watches, so he had no time for me at all," said Joanne. "I would want to talk about it and he couldn't understand that I was upset. He would take everything I said literally and tell me 'if you're not happy, it was a big mistake and we'll just get divorced.' But I just wanted to know what was wrong." The low point was a weekend break in Florida. "We stood on a bridge and discussed financially what we'd do if we got divorced. Although there was a lot of equity in the house, he was completely and utterly prepared to give it all to me. No questions. I looked at him and thought: you do love me but there's something weird about you."

As it turned out, Sebastian was on the autism spectrum and found it hard to read body language and had poor social skills. However, I tell the story because Sebastian's generosity broke through their crisis and the couple are still happily married ten years later. Even if your relationship is ticking along reasonably happily, being generous and making the first move—without worrying who is giving the most—can start a revolution.

Compassion is useful because it helps us cross over any gender differences and value our partner's take on important issues. For example, I counsel many couples who have different interpretations of what constitutes intimacy. "I'm not asking for much," said Amber, thirty-seven, "just not to be taken for granted, to be told I love you without having to ask, and those little gestures that show he cares." Her husband, Dieter, seemed to want the polar opposite: "But I want an easy, comfortable relationship where I feel secure enough to take love for granted, where I don't have to be always checking how it is going." They had been dismissing each other's needs by complaining "he's a typical man" or "I just don't understand women." However, when they were compassionate and found a way through the cynicism, they discovered that their particular form of intimacy did not exclude their partners. Amber admitted "I love the simple warmth of lying next to Dieter and hearing his companionable heartbeat." And Dieter accepted: "I like feedback and reassurance too."

Finally, going beyond cynicism allows hope to flourish. This is ultimately the most important ingredient for a successful relationship. During the dark moments, we need hope that things will get better. It also helps us believe that love is something more than a business deal where you agree to one set of things and your partner another.

## EXERCISE  THE MOST IMPORTANT EXERCISE OF ALL

It is hard to be generous, compassionate, and hold on to hope. Sometimes making the first move is such a giant leap of faith that I reassure my clients and say: just experiment.

- Rather than making a commitment to do something forever, just experiment—once, twice, or maybe for a week.

- At the end of your short time frame, reassess your progress.

- If you are generous, compassionate, and enter the experiment full of hope, I guarantee that things will not be worse. Most likely, they will be a whole lot better.

- Finally, look back through the book and think about the exercises or ideas that you would like to adopt but which seemed too hard. Why not experiment and try them for a week too?

I did this exercise with Janet, forty-eight, whose husband had left, asking for "time to sort myself out." Rather than taking the heat off their problems, it had made things worse and the couple would fire angry texts back and forth. I asked Janet to experiment and find out what would happen if she sent only nice texts for a week—after all, she wanted to repair their relationship and for her husband to return home.

Janet returned a week later, all smiles. Her husband had sent a text full of swear words and recriminations about the amount of money she had spent decorating the house. However, she kept her calm and had texted back: "I understand that you're angry but painting is the only thing that's kept me sane. I miss you. Janet." When he bought their daughter a cell phone, even though they had previously agreed she wasn't old enough, Janet bit her tongue, and said nothing. "How has the experiment gone?" I asked. "It took quite a bit of self-restraint but I didn't wind myself up composing nasty texts. Better still, I didn't have to cope with all his angry replies. So not only have we been getting on better, but I've felt better in myself."

## FIND A BETTER UNDERSTANDING OF LOVE

When couples who have grown and changed look back at their journey, remember the knowledge acquired and the new skills learned, they find a lasting belief in themselves. So what is this knowledge?

- ❦ Love is effort. In a good relationship, both partners regularly and routinely attend to each other's needs—no matter how they feel. This extra mile is often what is most appreciated.

- ❦ Love is about both giving and receiving. In a good relationship, both partners make certain they find the joy in both halves of the equation.

- ❦ Love is courage. In a good relationship, both partners share their vulnerabilities as well as their strengths and do not close themselves off, shut down, or take the easy option.

- Love is rewarding. In a good relationship, both partners support each other and help each other grow.

- Love is most appreciated when a couple thought it was lost forever, but have subsequently found a way back to each other again.

- What about the skills learned?

- To be honest with oneself.

- To be honest with your partner.

- To be up-front about differences, rather than ignoring or hiding them away.

- To negotiate better.

- To find a genuine compromise, rather than one partner just backing down or steamrolling over the other.

## SUMMING UP

These love hacks build on and reinforce each other, and over time will transform your relationship. If you "understand the pattern" of disputes with your partner, you will move beyond blaming each other. This will make it easier to "have fun together" and to discover a "third way" around difficult arguments. By "accepting what you can't change" and "going beyond cynicism," you will "find a better understanding of love."

## IN A NUTSHELL:

- Talking about an argument seldom makes it worse.

- Tolerating and forgiving your partner's failings makes it easier to accept your own.

- Love is about giving and receiving.

# Further Reading

## *I Love You, But I'm Not In Love With You*

Over 100,000 copies sold worldwide. This book will help you get to the roots of why seemingly loving partners detach and how the simple everyday things you thought were protecting your relationship were really undermining it. Also includes:

- How to argue productively and address the core of the issue.
- Employ the trigger words for more effective communication.
- Find a balance between being fulfilled as an individual and being one half of a couple.
- Create new bonds instead of searching for old ones.

### Have the Sex You Want

If your sex life is more about going through the motions than building connection, this book is for you. It features my step-by-step guide to bringing back the intimacy into your relationship and having the more-connected sex you have always dreamed about. It also includes:

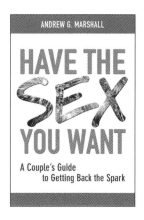

🌱 Deal with different levels of desire.

🌱 Combat the unhelpful myths about men and women and sex.

🌱 Repair the damage from an affair by reconnecting again in the bedroom.

### Wake Up and Change Your Life

If your problems are more fundamental, I have nine ideas that build into a proven plan for personal transformation (which in turn could transform your relationship). There's an explanation of why change is so tough and how to discover what's really holding you back. Most important, for when you're in crisis, there's advice on how to keep calm. The book also features:

🌱 Everything you need to know about improving the way that you communicate.

🌱 The importance of boundaries for you and your relationships.

🌱 Understanding the difference between your zone of concern and your zone of control.

🌱 An in-depth explanation about mindfulness and living in the present.

## *How Can I Ever Trust You Again?*

If your partner has had affair, my best-selling book covers the seven stages of recovery. It will help make sense of your feelings and reassure that they are normal and understandable. There's also my detailed plan on how to come out of this crisis with a stronger and better marriage. Each chapter ends with a short section written for the partner who has been unfaithful and many couples find these prompt constructive conversations on how to move forward. The book also includes:

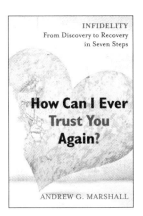

- 🌱 The eight types of affairs and how understanding your partner's is key to rescuing your relationship.

- 🌱 How to stop your imagination running wild and your brain going into meltdown.

- 🌱 How the person who had the affair can help their partner recover.

- 🌱 What derails recovery and how to get your marriage on track again.

## *It's Not a Midlife Crisis,*
## *It's an Opportunity*

If you think your partner is having a midlife crisis, but even suggesting the idea makes him or her angry and resentful, you'll find this book really helpful. If it's your life that no longer makes sense and you're looking to make big changes, it will help you take stock, understand how you got to this place, and make a considered plan for the future. Whichever side of the divide you stand, this book offers:

💗 A whole new vocabulary for discussing the midlife crisis without alienating each other.

💗 What causes depression and what is a helpful and an unhelpful reaction.

💗 Five killer replies to the blocks that stop you talking properly about your marriage.

💗 Why if you pass the midlife test everything is up from here.

# About the Author

**Andrew G. Marshall** is a marital therapist with over thirty years' experience. He trained with RELATE (the UK's leading couple counseling charity) but now leads a team in private practice in London and Berlin offering the Marshall Method. He is also the author of nineteen books on relationships and contributes to *Mail on Sunday, Sunday Telegraph, Times,* and women's magazines around the world. To date, his work has been translated into over twenty different languages. You can follow Andrew on Twitter and Facebook, but to receive regular updates about his books, articles, and events, subscribe to his newsletter at www.andrewgmarshall.com.